PRUSSIA:
the history of a
lost state

RUDOLF VON THADDEN

Translated by Angi Rutter

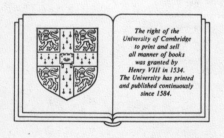

The right of the
University of Cambridge
to print and sell
all manner of books
was granted by
Henry VIII in 1534.
The University has printed
and published continuously
since 1584.

Cambridge University Press

Cambridge
London · New York · New Rochelle · Melbourne · Sydney

Editions de la Maison des Sciences de l'Homme
Paris

Published by the Press Syndicate of the University of Cambridge
The Pitt Building, Trumpington Street, Cambridge CB2 IRP
32 East 57th Street, New York, NY 10022, USA
10 Stamford Road, Oakleigh, Melbourne 3166, Australia
and Editions de la Maison des Sciences de l'Homme
54 Boulevard Raspail, 75270 Paris Cedex 06

Originally published in German as *Fragen an Preussen* by Verlag C. H.
Beck München 1981 and © C. H. Beck'sche Verlagsbuchhandlung
(Oscar Beck) München 1981.
First published in English by Editions de la Maison des Sciences de
l'Homme and Cambridge University Press 1987 as *Prussia: the history of a
lost state*
English translation © Maison des Sciences de l'Homme and Cambridge
University Press 1987

Printed in Great Britain at the University Press, Cambridge

British Library cataloguing in publication data

Thadden, Rudolf Von
Prussia: the history of a lost state.
1. Prussia (Germany) – History
I. Title
943   DD347

Library of Congress cataloguing in publication data

Thadden, Rudolf von.
Prussia: the history of a lost state.
Translation of: Fragen an Preussen.
Includes bibiography and index.
1. Prussia (Germany) – History. I. Title.
DD347.T4713 1987   943   86-24466

ISBN 0 521 30417 2
ISBN 2 7351 0176 2 (France only)

PRUSSIA: *the history of a lost state*

'What it boils down to today is whether you are prepared to accept an historical reality, or whether you want to go on believing what you wish to. It is a fact that the victor powers, exploiting anti-Prussian feeling rife throughout the world, have now erased the name of Prussia from the map of European states. But there is currently no point in questioning the political wisdom of this action, or in asking whether it was justified . . . Now that we are subject to the victors' authority, there can be no question of salvaging the concept of Prussia as a state. Given the general mood prevailing throughout the world, that would be a hopeless task in any case. At best, one can try to encourage historians to judge Prussia fairly, on the basis of the facts. For that, however, the political atmosphere has not yet been sufficiently cleansed of its poison. The whole disaster, which Nazi criminals inflicted upon Germany and the rest of the world, is being blamed on Prussia, regardless of the true facts. Thus, my dear Count, we shall have to be patient.'

(Otto Braun, in a letter dated 8.4.1947, written in Ascona to the former German National People's Party (DNVP) deputy and *Reich* Minister of Agriculture, Count Kanitz.)

Contents

Foreword

It is forty years since the state of Prussia officially ceased to exist, and yet once more it has become a controversial topic. There are questions to be asked, not only because the subject-matter remains problematical, but also because opinions are highly divided as to how far Prussian history is relevant to us today.

What is not in dispute is the fact that this history *does* affect us, for in both the postwar German states there is a feeling that Prussia represents 'part of our history', that it has left its 'traces' on the road leading to our present[1]. Although neither the FRG nor the GDR regard themselves as actual successors to what was once Prussia, they each compete with one another in laying claim at least to its cultural legacy. The West Berlin Prussian Cultural Foundation is confronted by a constant stream of counter-claims by East Berlin.

There are further illustrations of how the Prussian past is still with us today. The major exhibition on Prussian history mounted in Berlin was burdened, more than any other historical exhibition of recent years, with expectations and anxieties extending beyond a purely academic framework. What was at issue here was not just style and quality of presentation. The driving forces and consequences of history itself were on trial. It was clear that some kind of evaluation would have to be attempted.

In strange contrast to this tangible sensitivity towards the subject of Prussia, however, its history is remarkably inaccessible. Apart from the usual difficulties encountered by everyone in search of past realities, here there are additional barriers, above all the fact that access to the East Elbian key regions of the Prussian State is so limited. With opportunities to explore the areas that were once Prussia so very restricted, it is extremely hard for us to advance our historical understanding. Again, access to Prussia's history is hindered by certain political considerations; Prussia was drawn more deeply than any other state into the abyss of nationalist megalomania, and also paid a higher penalty than the others. In order to reach the deeper strata of historical reality, one first has to clear some kind of path through the rubble.

This book therefore attempts to make Prussia's history more accessible. Starting with comparatively straightforward questions of periodisation and geographical location, it proceeds to examine Prussia's social structure, its political character, its relations with Germany, its relations with Europe and, finally, its church history. Particular attention is paid to the way in which these individual elements have changed during the various historical epochs. In this way, it should become apparent that there can be no definitive statements about 'the nature of Prussia' valid for all time; instead, there are specific characteristics and experiences changing through time, although of course certain dominant trends may also be seen to emerge.

As long as the state of Prussia existed, every generation and every social or political grouping was able to have its own experience of Prussia and its own appropriate response, ranging from enthusiastic appreciation to embittered rejection. No such opportunity is available to us today. Nevertheless, the final chapter of this book attempts to assess Prussia's current significance. The various perspectives of – and motives behind – a newly-awakening interest in Prussia are discussed, with reference also to the problems of historical awareness in postwar Germany. Prussia is approached here not just as an object of historical enquiry, but also as a focus of the problem of establishing one's historical identity.

Following on from a series broadcast on North German Radio

(*Norddeutscher Rundfunk*) in 1979 (from which chapters one to
four of this book are taken), all the chapter headings are
formulated as questions. Correspondingly, the German edition
is entitled *Fragen an Preussen* (Questions about Prussia), meaning
questions addressing both the land and the people, questions
helping us towards a better understanding of a state in which
aspects of 'belonging' always played an important role. Beyond
this, the particular nature of Prussia's demise necessitates
certain questions: it was '*aufgehoben*', a word with three meanings
given to it by Hegel in his interpretation of dialectical historical
progress.

First, the Prussian State was 'dissolved', in the sense of
'abolished' '*aboli*', according to the English and the French text
of the Decree passed by the Allied Control Council on 25
February 1947. Second, it was 'elevated' during the final phase
of its history, raised to the higher level of the German *Reich*,
inextricably sharing in its fate. Finally, it was 'preserved',
retained as an unsuppressable element within our historical
consciousness.

As an object of historical research, Prussia invites certain
questions about itself; as a factor of political consciousness, it also
invites certain questions; we must address these questions if we
are to avoid running the risk of having no historical orientation
to guide us through the post-Prussian age. Precisely because
Prussia has been dissolved irrevocably and because there can be
no question of its being restored, it can remind us that, when it
emerges from the twentieth century, our world will have
changed considerably from what it was when it first entered this
century. Prussia can help us towards a better understanding of
the serious message of history: there are very firm limits as to
how much we can use it today, and yet there is still one thing
that is worthwhile preserving, namely an awareness of the
unique role played by Prussia in ushering Germany into the
modern world.

Chronology

1226	Proclamation of the Golden Bull of Rimini, authorizing the Teutonic Order to conquer and to proselytize the tribal land of the *Pruzzen*, east of the River Vistula.
1415	Mark Brandenburg passes, together with the Electoral title, to the House of Hohenzollern.
1466	Treaty of Thorn: the Order surrenders West Prussia to King Casimir of Poland, and the Grand Master recognises Polish sovereignty over East Prussia.
1506	University of Frankfurt/Oder founded.
1525	The Order's eastern lands around Königsberg become the secular Dukedom of Prussia, adopting the Lutheran faith.
1539	Introduction of the Lutheran Reformation in Mark Brandenburg.
1544	University of Königsberg founded.
1613	Prince Johann Sigismund is converted to Calvinism.
1614	Treaty of Xanten: Cleves, Mark and Ravensberg pass to Brandenburg.
1618	Brandenburg inherits the Dukedom of Prussia.
1648	Treaty of Westphalia: Brandenburg acquires part of Pomerania, the bishoprics of Halberstadt and Minden, as well as a claim to Magdeburg.
1660	Treaty of Oliva: Brandenburg acquires full sovereignty over the Dukedom of Prussia.
1675	Victory over the Swedes at Fehrbellin.
1685	Frederick William, the Great Elector, proclaims the Edict of Potsdam, offering sanctuary in Brandenburg to the Huguenots.
1694	University of Halle founded.
1700	Berlin Academy of Sciences founded.

1701	The Elector of Brandenburg is crowned 'King in Prussia'.
1720	Treaty of Stockholm: Stettin and the Oder estuary pass to Prussia.
1723	The General Directory is established as the highest administrative authority in Prussia.
1740/42	First Silesian War: Silesia is taken by Prussia.
1744/5	Second Silesian War.
1756/63	Seven Years War, concluded by the Treaty of Hubertusberg. Prussia retains Silesia.
1772	First partition of Poland: West Prussia (excluding Danzig and Thorn) and the Ermland are taken by Prussia.
1793	Second partition of Poland: Poznan, Danzig and Thorn pass to Prussia.
1794	Promulgation of the Prussian Legal Code.
1795	Third partition of Poland: territory around Warsaw and as far as the Niemen passes to Prussia.
1806	Defeat by Napoleon's armies at Jena and Auerstedt.
1807	Treaty of Tilsit: Prussia surrenders all lands west of the River Elbe, together with acquisitions from the second and third partitions of Poland.
1807/13	Era of Stein–Hardenberg reforms.
1810	Universities of Berlin and Breslau founded.
1814/15	Congress of Vienna: Prussia regains the province of Poznan and acquires Northern Saxony, together with Westphalia and the Rhineland as far as Saarbrücken.
1817	Establishment of Lutheran–Calvinist Union.
1818	University of Bonn founded.
1833	German Customs Union (excluding Austria) founded.
1847	United *Landtag* convened.
1848	Revolution in Berlin. A constitution is imposed.
1850	Treaty of Olmütz: Prussia renounces its policy of union with Germany.
1862	With conflict raging over the issue of a Constitution, Otto von Bismarck becomes Prime Minister of Prussia.
1864	War with Denmark over Schleswig Holstein.
1866	War with Austria for supremacy within Germany; Austria is no longer involved in the process of German unification. Hanover, Kurhessen, Nassau and Frankfurt/Main are acquired by Prussia.

1870/71	War with France is followed by the founding of the German Empire. The King of Prussia is proclaimed German Emperor.
1878	Anti-socialist laws are passed, in an attempt to quash the labour movement.
1890	Bismarck is dismissed from office.
1914	Outbreak of the First World War.
1918	End of the monarchies in Germany. Prussia becomes a free, Republican state.
1920	Otto Braun becomes Prime Minister of Prussia.
1932	Anti-Prussia coup d'etat by the *Reich* government: The last constitutional Prussian government, headed by Otto Braun, is deposed.
1933	National Socialist laws are passed to standardize (*gleichschalten*) *Reich* and *Länder*.
1939	Outbreak of Second World War.
1944	Assassination attempt upon Hitler.
1945	Following the conquest of Prussia's eastern territories by the Red Army, vast numbers of the German population flee. Those remaining are in subsequent years 'resettled' as decreed by the Potsdam Conference.
1947	The state of Prussia is formally dissolved by legislation passed by the Allied Control Commission.

Brandenburg–Prussian rulers since the early seventeenth century

Elector Johann Sigismund	1608–1619
Elector George William	1619–1640
Frederick William, the Great Elector	1640–1688
Elector Frederick III, from 1701 King Frederick I	1688–1713
King Frederick William I	1713–1740
King Frederick II, known as Frederick the Great	1740–1786
King Frederick William II	1786–1797
King Frederick William III	1797–1840
King Frederick William IV	1840–1861
King William I, from 1871 German Emperor	1861–1888
Emperor Frederick III	1888
Emperor William II	1888–1918

Historical maps of Brandenburg–Prussia

The maps depict the main features of Brandenburg–Prussia's territorial development. Accordingly, several details have been omitted, such as the temporary ownership of Neuchâtel in Switzerland.

Map 1 The Electorate Brandenburg at the time of its acquisition by the Hohenzollerns in 1415. At the time of the Reformation, the New Mark (shaded dark grey) also became part of Prussia.

Map 2 Brandenburg–Prussia at the time of the Great Elector (1640–88). The areas acquired during the Treaty of Westphalia are marked.

Map 3 The Kingdom of Prussia at the time of Frederick the Great (1740–86). The additional areas which he acquired are marked.

Map 4 Prussia during the reign of Frederick William II, showing the territories taken during the second and third partitions of Poland (shaded in dark grey).

Map 5 Prussia during the nineteenth century, following the Congress of Vienna (1815). The new acquisitions are marked.

Map 6 Prussia at the time of the *Kaiserreich* 1871–1918. The territories acquired by Bismarck during the wars of unification are marked.

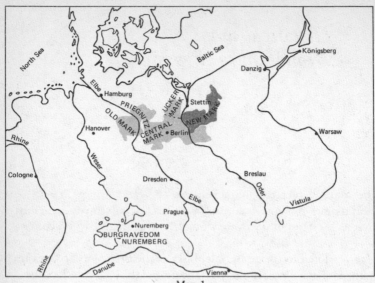

Map 1

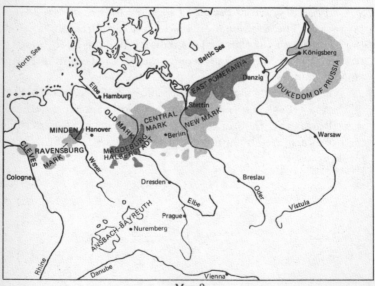

Map 2

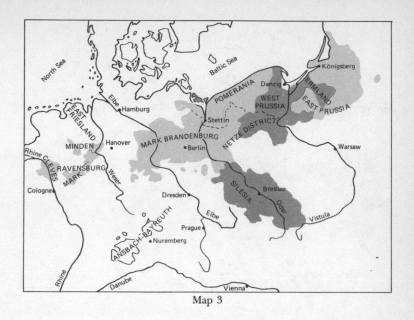

Map 3

Map 4

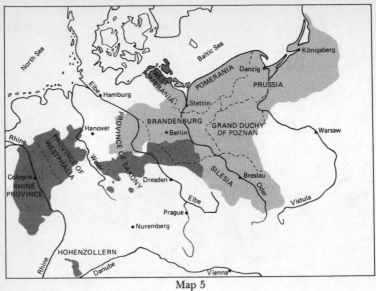

Map 5

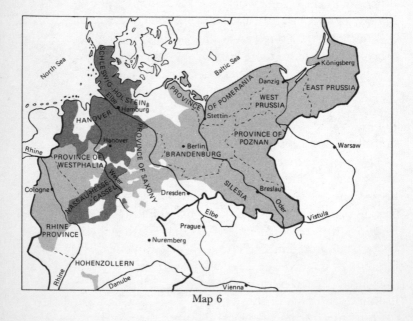

Map 6

1 ✦ *PRUSSIA: when was it?*

There are still several million people alive today who were born in Prussia, who grew up there and have first-hand recollections of many events in Prussian history. Yet this chapter asks a fundamental question as to the actual dates of Prussia's existence. It may perhaps seem obvious that Prussia's history extends to the threshhold of our own day, almost close enough to touch. Equally, it may seem futile to seek the very beginnings of Prussia's history, for these are surely located – like those of most other countries – somewhere in the Middle Ages, beyond the bounds of what we call 'the modern age'.

It may be that we tend to shelve this question in favour of others we consider more important to our understanding of Prussian history. It may also be, however, that we shy away from it because of its sheer finality. In seeking to determine a beginning and an end to any given phenomenon, we presume it to be a completed process, spent or defunct. Can the same be said of Prussia's history? Is it all over and done with?

This basic question is actually highly complex. Any historian knows that a nation's history can be completed; Prussian history, however, is not so easily 'written off', for it retains a certain proximity to us today. Unlike the history of the Roman Empire, or that of the medieval Norman State in Sicily, Prussian history continues to exercise a direct influence on us today, forcing us to examine a number of issues of contemporary relevance. The wealth of recent publications on Prussia is in itself a good proof of this.[1]

Quite apart from the vexed question of objectivity *vis-à-vis* a relatively recent period of history, an attempt to determine Prussia's beginning and ending raises problems affecting people other than just professional historians. Are there such things as hard-and-fast rules for establishing beginnings and endings in history, or are these more or less arbitrary assumptions, full of historical prejudices? Prussia's history is an excellent illustration of how the decisions involved in periodisation are far from immaterial.

Let us start with the problem of pinpointing Prussia's beginning. Many historians equate this with the development of the Teutonic Order at the height of the Middle Ages, thereby including the colonisation history of what was later Eastern Germany.[2] They argue that the subsequent Kingdom of Prussia owed not just its name, but also its royal foundations, to the Teutonic land on the lower reaches of the River Vistula. Without the land originally inhabited by the *Pruzzen*, as the tribe was known, Prussia would never have acquired the name *Preussen*, nor would it have been able to exercise decisive influence from outside the Holy Roman Empire of the German Nation, founding a new monarchy in opposition to the Empire of Vienna.

But we must now ask whether there is any relationship of continuity between medieval Prussia and the modern Kingdom of Prussia? Are the two not only centuries apart but also worlds apart? Is there a genuine historical link between them, or is this merely an artificial projection, made with the benefit of hindsight? One does not have to be a particularly expert historian to sense the dangers of indulging in this kind of historical construction. To do so is not only to exaggerate the significance of just one part of the subsequent monarchy, but also to open the floodgates to all kinds of Prussian myths, not least that of Prussia's 'Eastern Mission'. Prussian history thereby acquires a certain emphasis which appears suspect, for example, to Polish observers.[3]

Other historians set the beginning of Prussia's history at 1415, when control of Brandenburg and, with it, one of the seven Electorates of the Holy Roman Empire, passed to the House of

Hohenzollern. Supporters of this view argue that Prussia was a Hohenzollern creation;[4] neither its terrain nor its inhabitants comprised a natural entity that could have been judged to be the very basis of its history as a state. Hence, Bismarck's emphasis – in Chapter 13 of his *Reflections and Reminiscences* – on the great importance of dynasties, as opposed to tribes,[5] was intended partly as a comment on the Prussian state.

Apart from the fact that 1415 is simply one date in the history of Brandenburg, with no relevance to the history of the other regions later comprising Prussia, there is a further danger hidden in this argument. By focussing on the issue of dynastic rule, one tends to lose sight of both the country and the actual people concerned. Indeed, the historian may paint a quite misleading picture of reality when suggesting that forms of dynastic rule inevitably reflect every aspect of life in a given place at any particular time.

A third possible beginning to Prussia's history is the reign of Electoral Prince Johann Sigismund at the start of the seventeenth century, a period which brought several important changes to the nature of the Hohenzollern state.[6] Three notable events took place. First, in 1613 the ruling House's conversion to Calvinism; then in 1614 the acquisition of the western areas of Cleves, Mark and Ravensberg; and in 1618 the succession in the Prussian Duchy east of the Vistula. All three episodes had vital consequences. The conversion to Calvinism alienated the Hohenzollern rulers from their predominantly Lutheran subjects, thus paving the way for absolutism; the acquisition of Cleves, Mark and Ravensberg forged links between Brandenburg and the western regions of Germany, drawing interest towards an ambitious Holland; the succession in the Prussian Duchy eventually led the Hohenzollerns into the web of east European politics and on the road to power in the Baltic.

The significance of these events has never been recognised and expressed more clearly than by the first renowned chronicler of Brandenburg–Prussian history: King Frederick II, known to posterity as Frederick 'The Great'. In his famous *Memorabilia on the History of the House of Brandenburg (Mémoires pour servir à l'histoire de la maison de Brandebourg)* of 1751, he demonstrated an admirable grasp of essentials:

In my opinion, only the things that are worth preserving deserve to be written down. That is why I have skipped through Brandenburg's obscure origins and the reigns of the first Princes, since they have little to offer of interest. Works of history are not unlike waterways: they only start to become significant once they are navigable. Brandenburg's history only begins to get interesting during the time of Johann Sigismund, with his acquisition of Prussia, and the Cleves succession, to which he was legally entitled by marriage. It is only from this point onwards that the subject matter becomes meaty enough, so to speak, for me to get my teeth into it properly.[7]

This view, convincing though it may be, is bound to provoke objections. Like every attempt at periodisation, it has something rather arbitrary about it. Quite clearly, Frederick was judging history on the basis of one of his own pet interests – the consolidation of state-awareness (or what might today be termed 'political consciousness') amongst the populations of the scattered terrains under his rule. It was therefore only natural for him to start his history with the reign of the first Electoral Prince to extend Hohenzollern rule beyond the boundaries of the Mark Brandenburg.

Yet Frederick's attempt to demarcate the start of 'note-worthy' Brandenburg–Prussian history achieved only limited success. For those who lived after him, truly patriotic enthusiasm for the Prussian fatherland was generated not by the old legendary hero Johann Sigismund but, instead, by the figure of the first ruler to exude dynamism in both domestic and foreign policy, the Great Elector. To Fontane, the Great Elector marked the real beginning of Prussian history, the Prussians being 'a people whose traditions have barely advanced since the days of Fehrbellin'.[8]

The list of dates possibly marking the beginning of Prussia's history would not be complete without mention of the 1701 Coronation.[9] This is the point at which the name 'Prussia' first moved into the centre of the royal title, indicating the Electoral Prince of Brandenburg's claim to areas beyond his own immediate territory. Thereafter, Brandenburgers and Rhine-landers were also able to call themselves Prussians, expressing a common consciousness of belonging to one state.

Naturally, some time had to elapse before the claim implicit in the royal title was actually fulfilled. Ultimately, it was the Seven Years' War and pride in the great King Frederick's achievements that finally bolstered a Prussian sense of community. The year 1701 had seen the formal prerequisites created, and it is therefore not unreasonable to regard the founding of the kingdom as the beginning of Prussian history proper.

It is, however, just as easy to advance several counter-arguments to this, notably the view that this is too radical a pruning of Prussia's past, leaving, in effect, little more than the eighteenth and nineteenth centuries. To exclude the seventeenth century is to tear up the all-important roots. Without the Empire's decline, and without the exhaustion – manifested in the Peace of Westphalia – of the old powers of Central Europe, Brandenburg–Prussia's ascent to the status of a new major power in Europe could never even have taken place, let alone be accounted for.[10]

A great deal depends, therefore, upon one's particular historical perspective. When looking at the local history of Prussia's important regions, one has to go right back to the height of the Middle Ages and examine Germany's colonisation of areas east of the River Elbe. If, in contrast, one is primarily concerned with the influence of Hohenzollern rule, then one will take its dynastic origins in Brandenburg and identify the various consistencies and inconsistencies in its pattern of development. If, again, one prefers to look at the emergence of the modern state in one of its purest forms – the rise of a new great power in Europe – then one will concentrate on the seventeenth and eighteenth centuries, treating the earlier ones as one would treat prehistory. Everything else is simply a matter of ideology.[11]

Establishing the origins of Prussian history poses quite considerable methodological problems from the outset. It is not any easier determining when it drew to a close – an equally important question which should not be neglected. It brings us into the nineteenth and twentieth centuries, encroaching upon the very threshold of our own age. By and large there are four possible dates for the end of Prussian history: 1871, when the new German *Reich* was founded; 1918, when the Hohenzollern monarchy fell from power; 1932, when von Papen led a *coup d'état* against the Republican government of Prussia; and lastly 1947, when the Allied Control Council decreed the abolition of the Prussian state. Each of the four possibilities can be justified; each of them, however, conceals certain dangers, as we shall see.

The first option is undoubtedly the hardest to defend.[12] It is true that in 1871, at Prussia's instigation, a new German *Reich* was founded; but the state of Prussia continued to exist. Although important areas of jurisdiction were transferred to the *Reich*, Prussia was neither dissolved nor absorbed. On the contrary, debates persisted throughout the entire imperial period as to which of the two wielded the greater influence over the other, Prussia or Germany. Indeed, in many quarters – and especially abroad – it seemed as though the new German *Reich* was in fact just an enlarged version of Great Prussia (*Grosspreussen*). The Prussian Prime Minister was usually Chancellor of the Reich, too, and although from the 1890s onwards, non-Prussians occasionally climbed to the highest imperial offices, Prussians were still dominant in every respect. Prussian members of the *Bundesrat* needed no recourse to their blocking minority in order to emphasise Prussia's political weight.

Nevertheless, after 1871 Prussia enjoyed less political autonomy than it had done previously, when it was a totally separate state. With the creation of the *Reich*, new agreements had been entered into, and these had certain repercussions upon Prussian *raison d'état*. Above all, its populace had been drawn helplessly into a maelstrom of nationalism. Despite frequent assertions of Prussian individuality, there was a growing tendency for people to regard themselves simply as 'Germans'. As the Empire underwent novel processes of industrialisation and economic integration, greater social mixing with other parts of Germany ensued. By the end of the imperial period, Prussian particularism had little more than a formal, institutional existence.

Thus the second option appears more convincing. It sets November 1918 as a clear end to Prussia's history, the end of the Hohenzollern monarchy and thus the end of many areas of Old-

Prussian influence.[13] The Weimar Republic ultimately continued the process of standardising the *Reich*, reducing the individual weight of earlier Federal States. Yet this theory overlooks the fact that – in spite of the above mentioned standardisation – individual states continued to exist as *Länder*, most notably Prussia, with its disproportionately large area. Although efforts were made by the constitutional lawyer Hugo Preuss to dissolve the Prussian state into provinces and to achieve a more equitable composition of the *Reich* on the basis of approximately equal-sized *Länder*, the National Assembly voted in 1919 for Prussia to remain just one independent *Land*.

This was not all. Prussia did not just survive into the Weimar Republic, it actually acquired new political weight of its own. With a social-democratic government, it enjoyed a measure of stability that was in stark contrast to the upheavals typical of *Reich* politics at that time. Furthermore, originally conservative in complexion, Prussia was now a bastion of the Republic, far better able to withstand attacks upon democracy than was the *Reich* as a whole.[14] For this reason, to conclude Prussian history with the fall of the Hohenzollern monarchy, stopping short of the Weimar period, would be foolishly myopic. It would be opting for a one-sided picture of the Prussian state as a profoundly conservative monarchy only, completely ignoring the Prussia that fathered so many intellectual traditions of the left.

Should we therefore choose the third option listed above, and view the collapse of the democratic experiment on the eve of Hitler's seizure of power as the end of Prussia's history? Was it not brought to a close on 20 July 1932, with Chancellor von Papen's dismissal of the last democratically-elected republican government in Prussia? Thereafter, there was nothing to stop Prussia, too, from being standardised (*gleichgeschaltet*) along Nazi lines.[15]

Undoubtedly, there are certain risks in determining Prussia's end on the basis of a legal technicality, the formal dismissal of the last democratically elected government. This event, wretched enough in itself, was followed by a crucial period in

Prussian–German history. The term 'Prussian–German' is fully intended here, since no amount of reference to Prussia's anti-fascist resistance can disguise the partly Prussian origins of Hitler's imperialism. Had he not had the instruments of the German *Machtstaat* – itself so deeply influenced by the Prussian example – at his disposal, the Austrian Hitler would not have been able to pursue his pernicious plans quite as far as he did. There can be no escaping this fact, although this is certainly not to suggest that Prussia's history be reduced to a prehistory of the so-called Third *Reich*.

Potsdam Day, when the elderly Prussian Field-Marshal von Hindenburg shook hands with the new Chancellor Adolf Hitler in the Garrison Church of Frederick the Great, is not only a date in German history. It is also a date in Prussian history.[16] Moreover, it should be remembered that, in their constant observance of Prussian traditions, and in claiming Prussian virtues for themselves, the National Socialists actually kept Prussia alive. To take 20 July 1932 as the conclusion of Prussia's history would, in effect, be an easy way of escaping our own history. Prussia's role in Hitler's Third *Reich* is an issue we cannot avoid.

There remains just the fourth, and final, possible conclusion to Prussian history; that suggested by the decree issued by the Control Council on 25 February 1947. On that day, Allied legislation formally dissolved the state of Prussia by striking it, as a legal entity, from the list of European states. The Allies wished Prussia to be held responsible for the aberrations of German history and to be condemned, above all, as the embodiment of militarism.[17]

Again, certain reservations arise, making these dates seem somewhat unsatisfactory. First, there is the problem of mere legal documents – already discussed with reference to 20 July 1932. We need recall only the period of German Idealism, when philosophers raised states – Prussia, especially – to the level of spiritual entities, and it is already difficult to believe that Prussia was eliminated with a single stroke of the pen. Secondly, it is possible that, on the day of the Control Council decision in 1947, the state of Prussia had in reality already ceased to exist, possessing only a modicum of territory. The majority of its east German land was by this time already owned by other states, whilst its central and west German provinces had in 1947 long been part of other German *Land* configurations. Prussia's official unity was already dead when the Allied Control Council pronounced its death sentence.

One final – and particularly crucial – reservation must be mentioned, concerning the realm of political consciousness. By the time it was officially dissolved on 25 February 1947, the Prussian state had long since faded from many people's political consciousness. The postwar German public was neither displeased nor delighted by the decree; at most, surprise was voiced that it had taken officialdom so long to catch up with history.[18]

We are thus faced with the peculiar phenomenon whereby this date too – relatively, the most plausible of all – represents a far from convincing conclusion to Prussia's history. As with the three other options, a sense of dissatisfaction persists, affecting not just the historian alone, with his abhorrence of ambiguity. We know full well that Prussia is dead and that it cannot be resurrected without being desecrated in the process.[19] Yet, without being able to indicate a precise date of death, we cannot give a satisfactory end to its history.

On balance, in attempting to date Prussia's history, we have not progressed much further than the writer Theodor Fontane. In his novel *Der Stechlin*, Pastor Lorenz remarks:

Looking back, we have three great epochs behind us – a fact we should never forget. The first – and perhaps the greatest – was ruled by the Soldier King. One cannot praise this man too highly. He was truly of his age and yet he was also ahead of his time. He not only brought stability to the kingdom, he also – more importantly – laid the foundations for a new age and replaced distraction, caprice and selfish ant-hill absolutism with order and justice. Justice, that was his best *rocher de bronze* . . . And then there came the second epoch, when a country which was dull both by nature and through its history, suddenly found itself shot through with genius. And then there came the third period, one which was not great and yet was also great. The country was wretched, suffering and half ruined. It was not genius that inspired the country at this time, but the people still shone with enthusiasm, with faith in a higher power, the power of the spirit, knowledge and freedom . . . And all that I have related encompassed a single century.[20]

2 ✦ PRUSSIA: where was it?

It may seem strange that our historical approach to a country in which a large proportion of our older generation once lived should question where that country actually was. Surely it is perfectly obvious that Bavaria is in the south, Westphalia in the west, Thuringia in the centre and Prussia in the east of Germany? And does it not follow that this has always been the case?

One needs, perhaps, to look at the changing map of Europe during the twentieth century to remember just how mobile territories and boundaries can be. Poland's position after the Second World War was different to the one it had occupied before the war, and prior to the First World War it was not marked on any map at all. Prussia, on the other hand, comprised a considerable area until 1914, particularly in the north and east of Central Europe, shrank somewhat after 1918, and then in 1945 disappeared from the map altogether. It is thus far from futile to ask the whereabouts of any given country.

This is especially true when the size and shape of a country offer some indications as to its character, which they may well have influenced in some way. Geography constitutes the basis of social and agricultural structures, and may even affect a considerable amount of foreign policy. If, as in the case of large parts of France, a country enjoys good soil and a favourable climate, it can develop a strong agrarian economy with appropriate material aspirations. If, however, like Prussia east of the Elbe, it has mainly barren soil, then its predominant ethos is likely to be derived from the values of frugality and modesty.

Equally, the relative strength or weakness of a nation's industrial and raw material base will also affect its economic attitudes.

Eighteenth-century civil servants were aware of this, and those in the Hohenzollern territories were particularly keen to promote what was called 'regional studies' (*Landeskunde*). Because they knew that the areas owned by their rulers were comparatively poor, they made a determined effort to disseminate their findings on Prussian economic and social conditions. It is thanks to these original endeavours that the modern study of statistics was developed.[1]

But it is not simply soil conditions which have a bearing upon the character of a given state; other geographical factors – such as transport links – can also affect it. A country comprising largely remote regions will develop differently from one served by major traffic routes. In Germany, for instance, access to Rhineland areas was always vital, for they contained the main routes from Italy to the Low Countries. The latter were the chief point of entry to the whole of western Europe. In concrete terms, Prussia was to be shaped by whether or not it extended as far as the Rhine, whether it was linked with the major arteries of the west, or whether it simply owned areas of little traffic in central and eastern Europe. Equally important was direct maritime access, with the possession of harbours and estuaries obviating the need to use transit routes across foreign territory. Such were the factors governing Prussia's potential image as a 'cosmopolitan' state.[2]

Lastly, there is the vital aspect of geographical consolidation. Under the old system of dynastic rule, it was by no means automatic for a state to possess a self-contained, solid block of land. More often than not, it owned a string of heterogeneous areas, each with different laws and constitutions according to the rights held by the individual territorial ruler. The length of their titles illustrate how complex ownership claims and rulers' rights were in these old European states.

This was very true of the Hohenzollern state, which was formed from quite separate territories. For instance: Frederick the Great was, among other things, King of Prussia, Margrave of Brandenburg, Duke of Pomerania, Magdeburg and Cleves, Prince (*Fürst*) of Minden and Halberstadt, Count of Mark and Ravensburg, Lord of Lauenburg and Bütow and, not least, Prince of Neuchâtel.[3] This array of titles and rights indicates just how heterogeneous Prussia's constituent elements were. These territories were far from uniform and in fact developed quite considerable centrifugal powers of their own. A desire for integration and alignment was therefore a dominant feature of Prussia's history, quite apart from the personal cravings for greater power cultivated by its individual princes and kings.

These are just some examples illustrating the importance of territorial area. Others, dating from the nineteenth and twentieth century, could be given, all pointing to the same conclusion: the geographical location of a state and its boundaries are significant, both historically and politically. Rather than list further instances, it must suffice to make a single statement, aimed directly at the most virulent Prussia-ideology to have emerged during the last 150 years, namely the idea that Prussia had a 'German Mission'. Many of the great nineteenth-century historians reinforced a view of Prussia whereby it was the Hohenzollern state's mission to bring about the unification of the German *Reich*. Furthermore, some even championed the notion that, in essence, Prussia had been specially constructed so as to restore to the German Empire the unity that had been shattered during the Middle Ages.

Hence the comment made by Johann Gustav Droysen, in the introduction to his multi-volume *History of Prussian Politics*:

What lies behind the founding of this state, sustaining and guiding it, is – if I may say so – an historical necessity. In this state, one side of our national life seeks or has already found expression, representation and standards . . . Prussia, too, encompasses only fragments of the German people and German lands. But what lies at the very core of this state is its mission for the whole, of which it has continually absorbed ever-greater parts. This mission is Prussia's *raison d'être* and its strength. If Prussia were able to forget it, it would cease to be a necessity. At all times, when Prussia did forget it, the state became weak, decaying and more than once close to disaster.[4]

The argument advanced here is that Prussian history has a deeper purpose: To lead the Germans out of inner disunity and towards reunification as one people. This view arose from the prevailing circumstances that cast Prussia very much in the key role within the unification process, not least on account of its geographical shape. A map of Germany on the eve of unification shows that Prussia fell into two parts: a fairly large area to the east of the Rivers Elbe, Oder and Vistula, with a smaller, but significant sector on the Rivers Rhine, Ruhr and Mosel. In between lay various non-Prussian territories, most notably Hanover, dividing Prussia's eastern regions from its western ones. Thus, Prussia already had domestic grounds for desiring greater territorial unity. What was more reasonable than for the other German states to pin their hopes for unity upon Prussia? In terms of its shape, nineteenth-century Prussia functioned rather like a vice gripping Germany, originally affecting only the area north of the River Main, but later acquiring more extensive influence.

Yet this process was by no means automatic and it was certainly nothing like an historical necessity. Only a few decades earlier, the map of Prussia had looked quite different, and, if there was any question of a 'mission', it was surely a Polish, rather than German one. At the turn of the eighteenth and nineteenth centuries, before the map of Europe was changed by the Napoleonic Wars, the Prussian state comprised almost more Polish than German land. Its centre of gravity was quite clearly east of the River Oder, embracing towns such as Warsaw, Lodz and Bialystok. At that time, since Prussia had acquired large areas through the partition of Poland, it seemed as though the Hohenzollern state was about to lose its focal point in Germany and adopt a course akin to that taken by the subsequent Austro-Hungarian monarchy. At all events, Prussia's German territory west of the River Elbe seemed, at that time, like the wretched appendages of a country swayed more by Polish than by German history.

Prussia was not overburdened with Polish territory for long, although – with Posen and West Prussia – Polish partition areas did remain an influential part of the Prussian state until the First World War. Nevertheless, this situation was important enough to illustrate the fact that the effect of Prussia's history is not restricted solely to Germany. More than any other European state, it concerns Poland, for both histories are almost fatefully intertwined. It is therefore no coincidence that current historical research in Poland is increasingly concerned with Prussian history, publishing a range of studies relating to various aspects of Prussia.[5]

Quite apart from the German–Polish issue, however, the question of Prussia's geographical location remains important. Even before the Polish partitions, Prussia's territorial shape underwent quite considerable change, showing that several developments were possible. During the early modern period, it was anything but certain that the Hohenzollern state would ever assume a position of supremacy within the Protestant north of Germany. A glance at the course of sixteenth-century history will remind us that Saxony seemed far more likely to dominate the Protestant camp and to establish a focal point north of the River Main.

This situation did not in fact change until the seventeenth century, once the Hohenzollerns – having inherited a whole string of estates – were in a position to extend their rule beyond the Mark Brandenburg. Above all, two acquisitions on the flanks of the subsequent German *Reich*, the Duchy of Prussia and the Jülich-Cleves inheritance on the Lower Rhine, helped to transform Prussia into a major state that stood out from the rest of Germany's territorial states. Even though the Hohenzollerns were still unable to compete with the Habsburgs and were far from being a European great power, they were nevertheless on their way to attaining a superior position in the Protestant north of central Europe. Their claim could be staked.

From the geographical point of view, however, these acquisitions initially caused Prussia nothing but headaches. Brandenburg, with Berlin its undisputed centre, was now joined by a variety of territories and mini-territories, none of them having the remotest connection with one another, and with their interests in no way governed by Berlin. Cleves on the lower Rhine was far more concerned with wealthy Holland than with impoverished Brandenburg, and in the Prussian area that lay between the River Vistula and Memel, there was more Swedish and Polish spoken than Brandenburg-German. Fortunately, additional acquisitions were made during the Peace of Westphalia – Minden in the west and the hinterland of Pomerania to the east – which helped to establish a link with the centre of the Mark Brandenburg. Without these, the original acquisitions might well have turned out to be a burden.

Nevertheless, the lands inherited during the seventeenth century led the way towards a Prussia no longer dominated by Brandenburg. The map of seventeenth-century Central Europe shows that the scattered parts of Hohenzollern territory were virtually crying out to be extended and amalgamated. They were thus the basis of a rapidly-growing desire for greater power. Positions now held on the Rhine and Memel rivers not only opened up all kinds of new geographical prospects, but also wrought qualitative changes to the level of political conscious-ness in Prussia: people were beginning to think not in purely regional terms, but in terms of the state as a whole.

But the first real breakthrough did not come until the eighteenth century, when the stage was set for Prussia's ascent to the status of a great power. As the century dawned, the great power Sweden was ousted by the newly-ascendent Russia; as the century drew to a close, Poland was wiped from the map with the help of the same Russia. By acquiring Silesia and West Prussia, the Hohenzollerns were able to establish a large, cohesive state, weighty enough to form a counterbalance to the first great power on German soil, Austria. Although the territorial basis may still have been a little too slight to sustain any independent policy as a great power, the glory of the great King Frederick was sufficient to ensure that Prussia would play a role in Europe, as well as in Germany.

Here again, geography dictated the style of the state. Without adequate territory, all attempts at grand-scale politics would have been utterly futile. No-one knew this better than Frederick the Great and, aware of Prussia's weakness, he set out to conquer Silesia and to acquire further territory. No-one knew better than Frederick, however, that for all its acquisitions, Prussia was still a great power on only a very narrow footing. When asked about Prussia's prospects, he once mockingly suggested that the official coat of arms include an ape, since Prussia was so good at aping the real great powers, without actually being one itself.[6]

Lastly, nineteenth-century Prussia was also keen to pursue certain logical consequences of its geography. As we have seen, in terms of foreign policy, it did this by taking on the German question as its own, incorporating its own annexation policies into the general drive for German unity. Bismarck's policy aimed to continue Frederick's legacy and to make Prussia into a truly great power.

Prussia's actual shape was to affect domestic policy for several decades, considerably hindering its parliamentary development. Its kings refused to allow a parliament for the entire state, arguing that their geographical situation was too problematical. What they feared was that a representative assembly of all citizens could well subject Prussia's highly heterogeneous social composition to intolerable frictions and conflicts of interest. On the eve of the 1848 Revolution, Frederick William IV addressed the United Diet, which he had convened belatedly and half-heartedly, as follows:

Prussia cannot tolerate this state of constitutional affairs. Why not?, you may ask. My answer is this: Take a look at the map of Europe, at the position of our own Kingdom and at our structural composition. Trace out our frontiers, assess the strength of our neighbours and, above all, bear in mind our history. God has seen fit to make Prussia great by means of the sword – outwardly, using the sword of warfare; inwardly, using the sword of the spirit and intellect. To be sure, this is not the negative spirit of our age, it is the spirit of order and of discipline . . . A military camp can be commanded by one will only, if the direst peril and greatest foolishness are to be avoided. By the same token, therefore, the fortunes of this land can be guided by one hand only, if it is to be spared an imminent plunge from greatness.[7]

There were, of course, other possible arguments. It was feasible to view Prussia's lack of geographical integrity as a pressing reason for greater consolidation, demanding that new bodies representing the entire state be set up. This was the background to calls made by liberal-democrats, such as the East Prussian

Johann Jacobi, that an Estates General or nationl parliament be
convened in Prussia, to safeguard it against fragmentation and
debilitation:

With 14 million inhabitants, and with its overall ability to put up a good fight,
Prussia – although surrounded by three Great Powers – can swing the balance
in whatever direction it favours. On account of this factor alone is Prussia
granted the compliment of being treated as an equal. What if Prussia were to
stand alone, however? Until now the unity of its people has been artificially
imposed, rather than growing naturally. Of its eight provinces, you can be
certain that not one would feel like a dismembered limb, if extraordinary
circumstances were to divide it from the others. No, from Saarlouis to the
Memel, our Kingdom knows no such unity. For this reason, any unilateral
development of a provincial Constitution *without* a national parliament would
be a threat to our future; instead of an organically-structured state, we would
have an aggregate of provinces, each concerned with its own special interests
only; our dear Fatherland would undergo – on a smaller scale – exactly what
we are witnessing in Germany as a whole: a decline in unity, together with
subjugation under foreign masters and a loss of civil liberty.[8]

From this angle, Prussian *raison d'état* dictated the establishment of a national representative assembly. It was not just a
reasonably tolerable constitutional concession, but, conversely,
a political imperative partly deriving from Prussia's geographical position. Indeed, one has to admit that, as a co-operative
effort between all the forces from 'Saarlouis to the Memel', a
pan-Prussian parliament would have been a powerful factor of
integration. The widely-scattered provinces would not then
have remained linked only by the crown, the bureaucracy and
the army, as was the case for long periods of the nineteenth
century.

One may thus conclude that throughout its history
Brandenburg–Prussia's geographical shape determined the
development of the state as a whole. Even though other factors
also came into play – above all, those relating to social and
economic structure – the fact remains that, at every given point,
Prussia's scope for manoeuvre was always prescribed by its
particular geographical contours. Basically, one could say that
the frequent territorial changes over time corresponded to
equally frequent changes of *raison d'état*. Although the ruling

dynasties maintained continuity in their interests, features of territorial discontinuity had a considerable impact upon Prussia's political self-image. There was a marked difference between just a small and impoverished electoral principality in Brandenburg, and a subsequent state stretching between the borders of France and Russia.

Seen from this point of view, the Hohenzollern state had at least five different shapes, all entailing various problems and features of political self-image. First of all, during the Reformation there was the Electoral Principality of Brandenburg, too small even to reach the Baltic, and lacking access to an estuary or harbour. At pains to avoid being drawn too far into the orbit of Saxony, the stronghold of the Reformation, Brandenburg chose, instead, to see itself as an impoverished, inhospitable colonial land.

Second, there was the seventeenth-century Hohenzollern state which acquired – by force of circumstances – a range of different territories, from the lower Rhineland to the River Memel. As a result, it was faced with the task of integrating these areas into one cohesive state. This not only furthered certain tendencies towards supra-regional policies, it also encouraged the beginnings of absolutist thinking on the part of the ruler, who then divested his provincial Estates (*Landstände*) of all political responsibility, accusing them of narrow provincial particularism. Above all, it led to dreams of a Protestant state, and to the belief that only through dynamic growth could this fulfill its mission.

Thirdly, there was eighteenth-century Prussia, which – partly due to its own achievements, and partly due to external circumstances – grew to become a major power in Europe, rivalling Austria. Following Sweden's collapse as a great power in the Baltic area, and parallel to the continuing decline in Poland's strength, Prussia acquired the chance of forming a larger, cohesive state occupying eastern and northern central Europe, grounds indeed for claiming to be a great power. With this, there arose the classic Prussian problem of available resources being overstretched. Accordingly, stringent rationalisation measures were effected in every area of public life, giving rise to what Sebastian Haffner aptly dubbed 'the tyranny of Reason'.[9] What developed was a state in which so-called secondary virtues such as willingness to serve and obligation to duty became important above all else.

Fourthly, towards the end of the eighteenth century, there was the great expansion of Prussian territory following the last partitions of Poland. This expansion threatened to change the whole character of the Prussian monarchy, transforming it – rather like the Habsburg monarchy – into a multi-national state, with its centre of gravity quite clearly situated to the east. This was not to be, however, since Napoleon altered not only the map of Prussia, but also that of all Europe, robbing the Hohenzollerns of their Polish and their German lands west of the River Elbe. For a time, Prussia was reduced to just its East Elbian region, unable to expand either eastwards or westwards, but focussed, instead, upon policies of domestic reform.

Fifthly, with the Congress of Vienna, Prussia finally acquired the shape that was to determine it for its longest period – the two-winged form so vital to the history of nineteenth-century German unification. The Rhineland areas provided a western and urban orientation, whilst the East Elbian provinces pointed to the eastern and rural world. In acquiring this dual shape, Prussia became entangled in one of the chief conflicts troubling every modern state in the process of industrialisation: the conflict between areas furthering industrial and political progress, and areas persisting with pre-industrial norms and lifestyles. Had Prussia remained limited solely to East Elbia, it would undoubtedly never have achieved German supremacy. It would also very likely not have alienated itself quite so radically from the Poles.[10]

At the end of Prussia's territorial history came the act which had a threefold effect – in the triple Hegelian sense of *aufheben* – upon the Hohenzollern state. Under Bismarck, Prussia's fate was irrevocably merged with that of Germany, and was therefore in one sense 'preserved', albeit having lost its own form and shape. It entered a greater, if not higher, form of statehood, and thus became 'elevated'. In so doing, however, it initiated the process of amalgamation which was ultimately to spell its formal 'dissolution'. And yet it lives on today in the form of a crucial question addressed to the German people, who still find it difficult to strike a reasonable balance between the requirements of state and national sentiments. Perhaps reflection on Prussia's volatile territorial history helps to prevent rigid and inflexible solutions, solutions which pay insufficient attention to the facts and which, paradoxically, therefore allow no room for manoeuvre or for change. Beyond this, Prussia's history can remind us that the 'German Question' has never been a question concerning just the Germans. On the contrary, it is firmly embedded within the history of the European nations, a history which – as was later to become apparent – also extends, via various ethnic groupings, to us today.

3 ✦ *PRUSSIA: who was it?*

It is well-known that during the years following the Second World War, anyone outside Germany who admitted to being Prussian could expect to meet with fairly hostile reactions. There was, however, one place where one could encounter surprisingly friendly sentiments: on the long promenade in the old quarter of Geneva, where a row of statues commemorates the great historical figures of the Reformation. Alongside Calvin, John Knox, William of Orange, Oliver Cromwell, Roger Williams and Gaspard de Coligny, there stands the Great Elector; adjacent, there is a text, chiselled in archaic German, which runs as follows:

We, Frederick William, make it known that, following the harsh persecution which has for some time been practised in the Kingdom of France against our co-religionists loyal to the Protestant Reformed faith, forcing many families to flee the Kingdom for other lands, we have been swayed by sympathy and thus graciously offer them a safe and free retreat into every corner of our lands and provinces.[1]

This is the text of the Potsdam Edict of 1685, with which Frederick William, the Great Elector, responded to Louis XIV's revocation of another edict – the Edict of Nantes – granting religious freedom to the Protestants of France. The Great Elector's Edict of Potsdam was to allow religious refugees being driven out of France – the so called Huguenots – to find a new home and to start life afresh in Brandenburg–Prussia. And indeed, they arrived in droves. From every part of France there came a stream of persecuted Protestants – noble officers and middle-class merchants, pastors and artisans, craftsmen and manufacturers. Although they scattered all over Prussia, there were also some areas of greater concentration. By about 1700, one in every three inhabitants of Berlin was French.[2]

This Huguenot Edict of Potsdam, proclaimed during the Great Elector's final years in power, marked the beginning of an important trend in Brandenburg–Prussian history. In contrast to that other act signed in Potsdam – the agreement between the victorious Allied Powers concluding the Second World War in August 1945 – this depicts Prussian history in a somewhat brighter light, or at least offers a different perspective. It opened the door to those being persecuted for their faith or their convictions, and set a precedent for a whole series of similarly humanitarian measures: the reception of Czech religious refugees from the Bohemian-Moravian regions subject to the Habsburg Counter-Reformation, the settlement of Salzburg refugees in sparsely-populated areas of East Prussia, and the opportunities given to every kind of 'colonist' and new citizen who wished – for economic or political reasons – to make a new start for themselves. There was a saying current at the time: 'No-one becomes a Prussian unless forced to by necessity, but having done so, they then thank God that they did'.[3]

The image of Prussia as a blessed and bountiful haven for settlers contrasts strongly with one which was to have far greater influence upon public opinion – the view of Prussia as a hidebound and bigoted Junker state, likely to stifle all forms of liberty with its complete 'lack of fresh air'. This was an image based, above all, on experiences dating from the nineteenth century, when ambitious strata of the urban population struck against the comparatively narrow social boundaries of an Estates-oriented society, conflicting with the nobility, whose position was especially strong in Prussia. The much-loathed Junker state became the epitome of a particularly militant ruling class, determined to preserve an outdated status quo, blocking the development of democracy. Even Theodor Fontane, whose writing – more than that of any other author –

immortalised the Prussian nobility, complained, in a letter of 1897:

Prussia – and, indirectly, all of Germany – is suffering under our East Elbians. We must pass over our nobility; we may visit it, as we visit the Egyptian Museum, and bow down before the Rameses and Amenophis. But our misfortune is to run the country so as to please the nobility, under the delusion that they are the only people living in it. As long as this situation persists, we can rule out any growth of Germany's might and reputation abroad. What our Emperor regards as *pillars* are in fact nothing more than *feet of clay*. We need a whole new set of foundations.[4]

Answers to the question 'Who was Prussia?' thus range from the view of Prussia as essentially a nation of colonists and immigrants, to that regarding Prussia as chiefly made up of Junkers and their underlings. The reality is somewhat more complex than this, however, and as with Prussia's territorial history, it may only be fully appreciated in the light of certain historical facts and figures. To begin with, there is the question of population size and growth. Again, as with Prussia's changing terrain, various answers are possible, but its development did proceed from modest beginnings to ultimately quite impressive dimensions. At the time when the Great Elector assumed power, Prussia was in the middle of the Thirty Years War. Wasted by poverty and starvation, some parts were actually depopulated. The Mark Brandenburg contained, in an area of about 40,000 square kilometres, appoximately 330,000 inhabitants, whilst Berlin was nothing more than a small provincial trading town of 10,000–12,000 people. Including the Brandenburg territories in Eastern Prussia and on the Lower Rhine, area and population were still only 80,000 square kilometres and approximately 650,000 inhabitants.[5]

By the time of the Great Elector's death, just after the Edict of Potsdam, Prussia had increased to 110,000 square kilometres, with the population reaching $1\frac{1}{2}$ million, despite the losses sustained during the Thirty Years War. The acquisition of territory in Pomerania, Minden and Halberstadt was un-doubtedly an instrumental factor in this growth, but it was also helped by increasing numbers of immigrants. Overall, the population had more than doubled. Two generations later, at the start of Frederick the Great's reign, Prussia had grown very little more in area, comprising barely 120,000 square kilometres. Its population had again almost doubled, standing at approximately 2,250,000. Towns were beginning to grow, too, although the great majority of the population still dwelt in the country. By the end of Frederick's reign, Prussia had undergone considerable expansion of both territory and population. With the addition of Silesia and Western Prussia, it now covered 195,000 square kilometres; the number of inhabitants had more than doubled, reaching almost $5\frac{1}{2}$ million by the year 1786. Figures for urban growth also indicate this trend: over 100,000 people were by now living in Berlin.[6]

During the nineteenth century, the figures suddenly jumped much higher, confirming Prussia's status as a great power, even in terms of its population. Thanks to the Congress of Vienna in 1815, Prussia grew to be 280,000 square kilometres, larger than the modern Federal Republic of Germany. At approximately $10\frac{1}{2}$ million, its population was twice what it had been at Frederick's death. Ultimately, after annexations were made during the Wars of Unification, Bismarck's Prussia occupied an area equivalent to that of the present FRG and GDR put together: almost 350,000 square kilometres, with $24\frac{1}{2}$ million inhabitants. Prussia thus became a force to reckon with within the *Kaiserreich*, since it thereafter contained over two-thirds of the total population.[7]

If we weigh up all these statistics, we are forced to conclude that they constitute a most extraordinary development. A population growth from $1\frac{1}{2}$ to $24\frac{1}{2}$ million people in the space of 200 years is astonishing, even allowing for the extra land acquisitions. Certain problems were bound to arise, above all that of integration. What bonds could there possibly be between a constant stream of immigrants and the state? What was it that made them feel Prussian, when they outnumbered the oldest generation of Prussians by 2:1, with the latter threatening to become a minority?

Theodor Fontane clearly recognised the problems resulting from such rapid population growth, and he analysed them with regard to the attendant social change. In his autobiographical sketch *From Twenty to Thirty*, he drew a comparison between conditions at the outbreak of the 1848 Revolution and those prevailing in Prussia under Frederick:

At that time, the Prussian nation did not yet exist. Our entire country consisted mainly of the East Elbian provinces, which were agricultural. These were peopled by nobles, the army and civil servants, and all other forms of human life – some four million souls lacking a soul – were deemed not to count. But, by the time Frederick William IV took over as ruler, nothing remained of the absolutist and patriarchal state of affairs that had prevailed at the dawn of the last century. Radical change had swept over everything. Four million people had become 24 million, and they were no longer *misera plebs*, but free agents, in spirit at least. Furthermore, they had not remained untouched by the shatteringly radical ideas of the French Revolution.[8]

Fontane thus saw how foolish it was to fall back on Old-Prussian traditions at a time when, in the wake of the upheavals wrought by the French Revolution, only a small sector of the population had been schooled within them. He recognised the problem of historical continuity, and was amused by the fictions of historical justification bearing no relation whatsoever to reality. Above all, he was irritated by the tendency towards self-delusion and the stubborn refusal to acknowledge that times were changing. This brings us to the second part of the question 'Who was Prussia?', and to the question of changes within the social structure. Here, too, the process that took place was as astonishingly rapid as was the population growth rate. It developed from a predominantly agrarian population, to be a modern industrial society, which was later to be crucial to the economic might of the state.[9]

Originally, there were just the 'farming provinces' mentioned by Fontane, without even the army or the bureaucracy. When the Great Elector assumed power, the land was backward and poor. It was a land of Junkers and peasants, where towns were of little significance, economic or otherwise. Social life was dominated by the squirearchy, a form of economic and social rule exclusive to eastern Germany and characterised by a specific kind of nobility. Unlike his noble counterpart in the west, the Prussian Junker did not lease off his lands, but instead worked them himself.[10]

This had several consequences: to begin with, it meant that the nobility was not ousted to the periphery of economic and social developments, but instead occupied a central position. Unlike the nobles of France, it did not turn its back on the countryside in favour of life at court. On the contrary, as a letter sent by Fontane to Friedlander suggests, it seemed to regard itself as the very countryside personified. Associated with this is another equally important consequence: the powerful position of the landed nobility, at the expense of East Elbia's towns which – after a heyday under the Hanseatic League during the Middle Ages – were undoubtedly worse off than other towns in the west of the *Reich*. The urban economy was for a long time milked by the agricultural estates, and it was precisely the small towns in the east which generally failed to grow much larger than smallholders' towns. In terms of political self-confidence, the latters' citizens were no match for the nobles and on the whole, they saw themselves as nothing more than simple country-dwellers. Lastly, the peasants were probably most affected by manorial rule. To them, an ever-present and actively farming master represented a far greater burden than did an absentee castle-owner; they had even fewer opportunities of resisting than the town-dwellers did.[11]

This was the background to Hohenzollern Prussia's entry into major politics – a social structure quite distinct from that of the western German territories. During the eighteenth century, however, subsequent developments helped to consolidate the bases of this structure. The nobility was joined by the two other forces mentioned by Fontane – the army and the bureaucracy, lending Prussia a whole new emphasis. Although the basic structure of 'agrarian provinces' remained, it was reorganised and rationalised, in the pursuit of higher aims. The army and the bureaucracy helped to break down the power of the Estates, but they did not erode the might of the Junkers, who were

proving themselves to be indispensible to the system of Enlightened Absolutism.[12]

The army and the bureaucracy not only served to re-stabilise
the nobility's position, they also opened up career opportunities
to men outside the aristocracy. It was above all the bureaucracy
which became a channel of entry for commoners, whilst a career
in the officer ranks remained, as a rule, the preserve of the
nobility. These new opportunities available to the commoner –
who could, of course, also enter into trade and commerce – did
little to foster the revival of self-confidence among the urban
middle classes, but instead merely created servility towards the
state. To a certain extent, this was no different to the military
service ethos prevalent amongst the nobility. Fontane was right
to complain, in a letter written in 1893, that Prussia under
Frederick had lacked both the 'citizen (*Bürger*) and the bourgeois, too'.[13]

The nineteenth century, however, introduced whole new
elements into Prussia's social structure. The acquisition of wide
areas of land on the rivers Rhine, Ruhr and Mosel boosted
Prussia's urban population, immediately prompting the question as to whether it was possible to integrate this into the old
state. Although the Stein–Hardenberg reforms of the East
Elbian provinces had advanced matters to some degree, the fact
remained that two completely different regions now belonged to
one and the same state – the east, predominantly agrarian, and
the west, predominantly urban.

Old-Prussian traditions were stubbornly clung to during the
nineteenth century, as claims to greater civil liberty were being
warded off from the newly-acquired western provinces. The
French Revolution had of course left its mark on the eastern
territories, but a real threat to the nobility would arise only if the
east were to unite with the heavily urbanised west. Moreover,
thanks to Frederick's social policies, the East Elbian nobility
enjoyed a far wider political function than many of their
brother-aristocrats did elsewhere in Europe. Accordingly, they
were all the more firmly entrenched. French critics of the
aristocracy had had an easier task than their Prussian counter-

parts, who were dealing with an Estate whose self-confidence
drew on the dual traditions of the active landowner and the state
civil servant.[14]

Middle-class writers often preferred to vent their criticism of
the nobility by depicting aristocratic figures found outside
Prussia. The Silesian Gustav Freytag – author of the novel *Soll
und Haben* (Debit and Credit), popular within middle-class
circles – illustrated the growth of middle-class self-confidence by
means of critical juxtaposition with the Polish aristocracy. In
this novel, two German businessmen discuss the insurgent
Poland of the 1830s. Of the Polish nobility, one of them
concludes that:

no other race is so incapable of making progress and of using their capital to
acquire greater humanity and education as the Slavs. What the leisured classes
have managed to acquire by oppressing the masses, is squandered on wild
frivolities. Here, this is the practice of certain privileged classes only, and the
nation can if necessary put up with it. But in Poland, a privileged few profess to
be representative of the entire nation, as though nobles and agrarian serfs
could together form one and the same state.

The second man replies: 'They have no middle classes',
whereupon the first continues: 'then they have no culture; it is
strange that they are incapable of creating the one class which
represents civilisation and progress, and which elevates a bunch
of disparate peasant farmers into a state'.[15]

Freytag is thus expressing – albeit from a somewhat dubious
perspective – the middle-class self-image, as distinct from a non-
Prussian aristocratic social type. Although he may well have
been thoroughly critical of individual members of the Prussian
nobility, he refrains from reducing them to mere ciphers of a
teetering *ancien régime* which evidently did not exist in this form
in Prussia. In Prussia, the fronts between the forces of progress
and of reaction were arranged slightly differently. The nobility
was growing closer to the middle classes than it was in Poland,
for example. Indeed, thanks to the service ethos developed
under Frederick the Great, the nobility was even quite useful to
the middle classes.

It was within this highly-charged atmosphere – with a

nobility firmly clasped to the bosom of the state, and with the middle classes 'domesticated' – that the Prussian labour movement had been developing since the turn of the century. It had no traditions to fall back on, neither middle-class strivings for emancipation nor aristocratic criticism of the state. Instead, it was obliged to seek out and establish a political position of its own. In that respect, even Frederick the Great seemed a commendable and memorable revolutionary, as far as some labour leaders were concerned. The most important example of this attitude was Lassalle, who – in spite of many reservations – regarded the great king and his state as marking a watershed. In 1858, in an essay on Lessing, he wrote:

In Germany, it was Frederick the Great who, in rejecting the old system of power relations, the *Kaiser* and the *Reich*, effected this reversal. This was no ordinary war over inconsequential issues such as territorial squabbles between Princes, this was – insurrection, mounted by the Marquis of Brandenburg . . . against the Imperial family, against all forms and traditions of the German *Reich* . . . insurrection which he pursued with the endurance and commitment of a genuine revolutionary . . .[16]

As a socialist, Lassalle was making a plea, albeit contestable, for Frederick the Great to be judged in a progressive light. This illustrates how impossible it is to answer the question 'Who was Prussia?' without referring to Prussia's left-wingers. Lassalle and his views were to come in for a great deal of criticism; so, too, were sympathisers such as Franz Mehring[17] and other Marxist socialists. Nevertheless, Lassalle demonstrated that Prussian history was in several ways associated with the growth of the labour movement. This was important, for in times of social unrest, the workers needed a position from which they could justify and defend their role within the Prussian state.

But the circumstances of Prussia's social structure meant that the task of politically educating labour was far from easy. Not only was there an arrangement for mutual defence agreed between the middle classes and the nobility, the Prussian state – governed, more than others, by the principle of social integration – was highly suspicious of emancipatory movements. Precisely because social development in Prussia was marked by so many contradictions, the authorities reacted all the more harshly, with policies of integration and suppppression. At the same time, though, these policies had the effect of making Prussia's labour movement a highly disciplined one, in marked contrast to those in other countries. Thus August Bebel pointed out to his French counterpart, Jean Jaurès, at the Amsterdam Congress of the Second International held in 1904, that the Prussian–German monarchy did have one good point. It may have lacked the parliamentary opportunities available in France's Third Republic, but it had seen advances in social policy which the French Republic could only dream of achieving.[18]

Prussia's old strata, however, were becoming less and less involved with social policy developments of this kind. Their agrarian nature granted them little understanding of the problems of industrialisation, and they were increasingly drawn towards ever-narrower policies of strictly agrarian interests. The one thing which had long enjoyed some legitimacy within their own East Elbian domain – the economic and social conservation of the rural environment and lifestyle – was now finally being shunted off into an economic and political siding.[19] Fontane was therefore right in complaining, in his letter of 1897, about the Junkers' outdated position, and in expressing a desire for complete social renewal in Prussia. His letter closes thus: 'It is extremely rare for states to collapse as the result of bold, though timely, reorganisation. I cannot think of a single such example. The reverse, however, has occurred hundreds of times'.[20]

In retrospect, therefore, we must ask why was it that Prussia, of all countries, was so incapable of social renewal, given the apparent mobility of its population and its comparatively receptive attitude towards new settlers? Beginning with Huguenots and colonists, it ended up with blinkered class-representatives and provincial politicians. How did this state of affairs come about?

One of the partly insoluble questions about Prussian history is the inter-relationship between breadth and narrowness. For example, there were wide-reaching territories housing the most petty-minded provincialism. There was extensive receptivity towards newcomers, and yet there was also much class-bigotry. There was a broad tolerance of various religious beliefs, and yet narrow pietism also prevailed. Lastly, there were a great number of versatile and commendable personages who were fervently proud of being Prussian, and yet there was also a great deal of meanness and narrow-mindedness which was partly, but not entirely, due to the circumstances of the time.[21]

Let us listen once more to Fontane, with the inimitable letter sent by the elderly Domina von Wutz, in the novel *Stechlin*, to her nephew Woldemar:

Even in this matter (of marriage), you must not abandon your homeland; you must, if at all possible, stay close to home. Even our own provinces can vary so enormously! I can see you smiling at my words of warning, but I assure you that I mean them quite seriously. The thing which I call nobility can still only be found in our Mark . . . You no doubt ask why I am . . . so very keen on our Mark or, more accurately, on our Mittelmark. The answer, my dear Woldemar, is very simple: In the Mittelmark, we do not just occupy a central position; we have also found a happy medium and maintain a central state of equilibrium, such an essential basis for every form of happiness. I therefore close with a request: Marry someone from home, and marry a Lutheran. And do not marry for money – money is degrading . . .[22]

4 ✦ *Prussia: what was it?*

Today, no-one asking 'What was Prussia?' can overlook a certain event in our recent history which was intended to – and indeed did – cause a great stir. It occurred on what is known as Potsdam Day, March 21 1933, when a few weeks after his seizure of power, Hitler publicly staged what he called 'the symbolic marriage of historic greatness and modern strength'. In Potsdam's Garrison Church, at the tomb of Frederick the Great, he invoked the spirit of the mighty king as an exercise in public relations, one might say, to inaugurate his new *Reich* with an appropriate degree of solemnity and legitimacy.[1]

Shrewd observers would have noticed how, in his speech, Hitler did not pursue the subject of 'Prussia' – indeed, not once did he even mention the name. His intentions were, however, clear from the context. Prussia's history was to be appropriated by the National Socialist *Reich*. Even then, there were some doubts on this score; after Hitler's regime collapsed in 1945, many historians were highly uneasy about failing to make a distinction between elements of Prussian history and elements of National Socialist history. Yet to a certain extent, this was justifiable, for even the most pro-Prussian historiographer cannot avoid admitting that precisely those who spoke so fondly of the so-called Prussian virtues were, in fact, paving the way towards Potsdam Day.

For example, Hugenberg – Chairman of the *Deutschnationale Volkspartei* – urged every Prussian-German sympathiser to join forces with the National Socialists and form the Harzburg Front. He conducted his anti-Weimar election campaign with

the help of posters depicting Frederick the Great, appealing to
what he imagined to be 'the Prussian Spirit' fighting against
democracy. In a speech given in Gleiwitz following the re-
election of the Prussian *Landtag* in April 1932, Hugenberg
uttered the slogan 'Prussia must become Prussian once again' –
which actually meant free from its democratic orientation. He
said:

Prussia is not a geographical concept, it is a moral conception of the state. No
matter how much its boundaries may have altered, one thing has remained
unchanged through the passing of time, and that is our moral conception of the
state, to which so many non-Prussians have become converted.[2]

Hugenberg was not the only person to emphasise the concept
of the state with regard to Prussia. Every right-wing thinker
since Hegel and Treitschke had held Prussia to be, above all, the
embodiment of statehood and order. In response to the question
'What was Prussia?', right-wingers would have had no hesi-
tation in answering 'a state, and nothing but a state'. They
would have emphasised everything related to the state and to its
order, everything which made it a governing principle of life.

This is what led Oswald Spengler – author of *The Decline of the
West*, a controversial work in its time – even to try to create a
synthesis between Prussianism and Socialism, a synthesis based
on what he presumed to be a common rejection of individualist
values. In 1920, under the explicit title 'Prussianism and
Socialism', he wrote:

German – or, more accurately, Prussian – instinct ruled that 'power belongs to
the whole, which the individual must serve'. The whole is sovereign. The King
is merely the highest servant of the state. Everyone has their own position to
occupy. Orders are given and are obeyed. Since the eighteenth century,
authoritative socialism has existed, basically illiberal and anti-democratic
when judged against the standards of English and French democracy.[3]

Here, therefore, Prussia acquires unmistakeable touches of
state Socialism. A direct link is established between the eighteenth and the twentieth centuries, between a century dominated by Frederick the Great and the century of Socialism. In so
doing, Spengler is blotting out all the values associated with the

nineteenth century, the era of Liberalism – values such as middle-class education, open attitudes of mind and the self-responsibility of the individual. As though he could skip over or block out the era that dawned with the French Revolution of 1789, Spengler tries to hold up Prussia as an anti-revolutionary alternative to the western European world so influenced by revolution, as an illustration of the direct continuity between old-style conservative attitudes to the state and modern, Socialist solidarity.

This kind of attempted equation of Prussian and Socialist positions was made not only by right-wing thinkers, but also by the left, even though the latter employed a quite different perspective. Ernst Niekisch, for example, the individualistic and – occasionally – anarchistic left-wing Socialist from Silesia saw Prussia as an ally in the struggle against bourgeois-capitalist society, an opinion he derived from observing history: 'The Prussian way of life', he wrote, during the early 1930s, 'was the complete antithesis of that of the burgher; militaristic, feudal and autocratic, the Prussian-German state was becoming increasingly intolerable to the *burgher*, for it went against his natural energies'.[4] Niekisch accordingly marked out the points of overlap in Prussian and Socialist development, all of which pointed away from the bourgeois world.

We are bound to ask, however, whether this is all there is to be said about the nature of Prussia. Is it generally valid to identify certain deficits in Prussia's middle-class culture and therefore to ascribe to it a special role in challenging the achievements of the bourgeois age: parliamentary democracy, the Liberal constitutional state and the capitalist economy? Before this question can be answered, it is essential to examine the course of Prussian history through time. It will become clear that – in spite of subsequent impressions – each epoch had its own answer to the question 'What was Prussia?' Although certain dominant trends mapped themselves out fairly early on, they were never so clear as to rule out all possibility of alternatives.

During the first significant era of Brandenburg–Prussian history – that of the Great Elector – the new state started to develop a certain characteristic of considerable consequence: its consciously Protestant orientation. There were other German territorial states that were Protestant; Brandenburg–Prussia, though, had one important distinction. Ever since the conversion of the Elector, Johann Sigismund in 1613, its ruling house was Calvinist and was therefore religiously alienated from the predominantly Lutheran people.[5] As a result, the Hohenzollerns were obliged to practice a policy of religious tolerance, in order to achieve a *modus vivendi* with their subjects. First, Lutherans and Calvinists, but also Catholics and, later on, Pietists were accorded political freedom in Prussia, so as to lessen the suffering caused by the religious wars.[6] Secondly, the Hohenzollerns' conversion to Calvinism helped them to mount more conscious resistance to the Counter-Reformation and to build a counterpole to the Catholic south of the *Reich*. Abandoning its Lutheran timidity, Brandenburg–Prussia became the focal point of an active Protestant spirit seeking to break out from the structural confines of medieval piety. Lastly, Calvinism furthered what might be termed the Hohenzollern state's emancipation from the *Reich*, i.e. the gradual, yet determined detaching of the young state from the fetters of the ageing Holy Roman Empire. No other German territorial state was at that time as relentless as Brandenburg–Prussia in its response to the weakness and the decay of the Empire. No other German state resisted as soberly and as realistically all romantic hopes for a revival of former imperial glory.[7]

Had one asked at that time 'What is Prussia?', one could have replied with an aphorism later coined by Fontane: Prussia is the state of the future.[8] In its standards, as well as its aims, Prussia represented a step forward from the Middle Ages, an advance towards new intellectual and political structures. Socially, it remained firmly anchored in the old world of Estates, but politically, it was beginning to break down their power: The state was to outstrip them, and become recognised as a vital dynamic force within the political domain, becoming increasingly ambitious and certainly more so than was society. It points towards a development which was later to be highly characteristic of Prussian history.

This bolstering of the state against the forces of society was to continue, coming to a peak during the eighteenth century. Under Frederick William I and Frederick the Great, every significant area of life was completely concentrated within state jurisdiction; the *Land* became nothing more than a recruiting ground for the state. Naturally, there were still areas of conflicting interest, and their individual autonomies were not done away with at a single stroke. Nonetheless, the general aim was to render these useful to the state wherever possible.

In concrete terms, the land of the great kings was swayed by two powerful influences: On the one hand, it was a state much determined by the army and by the bureaucracy, where the values of Reason and Order reigned supreme, with discipline and obedience necessary in all things, right down to the smallest detail. On the other hand, it was an enlightened state, subject to the rule of law, one which introduced the General Legal Code of 1794 and also created the preconditions for educational reform. The two sides are not as self-contradictory as they might appear; together, they ultimately form the basis of the modern state, which was also beginning to emerge in other parts of Europe. In Prussia, however, its development was particularly consistent; it advanced with an oppressive perfection that threatened to run away with itself.[9]

By the end of the eighteenth century, so crucial a century in Prussian history, a good number of answers had been given to the question 'What is Prussia?'. The fame of the ambitious Hohenzollern state had spread throughout Europe. Writers and philosophers were devoting their minds to it. The great French thinker Alexis de Tocqueville later called Prussia the remarkable combination of 'a modern head' upon an 'old Franconian rump', referring to that striking dualism of political modernity and social retardation which sometimes made Frederick's state appear so hybrid.[10]

To critical observers, however, Prussia seemed just like a barrack-yard, since military matters always took precedence over civilian affairs. Indeed, there was always supposed to be something rather disparaging about the term 'civilian' in Prussia. The most famous remark in this context is often attributed to the French Count Mirabeau, the great statesman of early revolutionary France, who visited Berlin and Potsdam shortly after the King's death: 'Other states have an army; Prussia is an army that has a state.'[11] A somewhat exaggerated judgement, to be sure, but misleading also in its suggestion that Prussia's generals held primacy over its statesmen, which was not the case. It is accurate only in that the Prussian state was, as Sebastian Haffner put it, 'obsessed with its concern for the army', if not with the army itself.[12]

Other commentators have been less critical, notably those who were impressed by the boost – material and spiritual – given to the Prussian monarchy. They focus their attention chiefly on the figure of the Great King, praising his personal contribution in the intellectual elevation of his people. Here, Goethe's maxim from *Poetry and Truth* is the most famous example of a sentiment shared by many of his contemporaries: 'Thus I grew favourably inclined towards Prussia or, more correctly, towards Fritz: We cared little about Prussia itself, it was the Great King's personality which moved us all.'[13] This attitude was to be one of the strongest influences upon intellectual circles in nineteenth-century Germany, an attitude which has frequently been the subject of Voltairean praise.[14] It caused the political balance of power to shift in favour of the state, rather than of society, making the state appear to be a guarantor of rational policy and an agent of necessary reform from above. Thereafter, the Prussian state was to hold a new, wider function. The French Revolution had changed the map of Europe and had established wholly new sets of standards; the question was now whether the state could forestall revolutionary demands and, by absorbing their content, defuse them. 'Revolution from above' became the motto of the day.

The key question relating to the nineteenth-century Prussian state is how far, if at all, it achieved this aim. Were its bold measures of reform from above sufficient to take the wind out of the sails of the revolutionary movement? Did its reform policy go far enough, so as to make revolution unnecessary? There can be no straightforward answer to this question. On the one hand,

the nation's best minds resolved that – because it had moder-
nised so rapidly during the eighteenth century – nineteenth-
century Prussia was to become a model of progress without
revolution. This was a view shared by prominent Prussians such
as von Humboldt, Stein, Hardenberg, Hegel and, with certain
reservations, Bismarck. On the other hand, the Prussian concept
of modernisation was now encountering several clear limitations. Previously, the Prussian state had had to contend only
with a backward, Estates-dominated society and had therefore
enjoyed a virtually unchallenged standing. Now, however, it
faced a nascent society which, in its anxiety to make progress,
was laying down its own new sets of standards. Prior to the
French Revolution, the word 'society' had been synonymous
with feudalism and the *ancien régime*. It was now coming to
connote democracy and civil rights.[15]

For the Prussian state, competing with these new social values
represented a novel and formidable task. This also explains why,
during the nineteenth century, it faced unprecedented challenges to its prestige. The ideas spawned by the French Revolution
were beginning to cast some very long shadows.

Initially, Prussia was able to maintain its position of strength
because the French Revolution itself appeared in the shape of a
foreign conqueror, Napoleon Bonaparte. Prussia sought to
counter his claim to power by using the strength of both social
reform and intellectual renewal. In the words of Wilhelm von
Humboldt, spoken during the infancy of the new University of
Berlin, 'the state shall make up for its material loss of strength by
acquiring new intellectual powers'.[16] This was a truly Prussian
statement, prompted by an acute awareness of a need for some
kind of compensation. It also illustrated an attitude that became
highly characteristic of Prussia's image during the period of
German Idealism: the elite, as distinct from the mass. It was
further reinforced by the feeling that Prussia had no mass – in
terms of either population or geography. In an essay on the
Prussian Almanachs, Wilhelm Dilthey later expressed this idea
as follows: 'Prussia's position is based not on natural conditions,
but on its intellectual vigour.'[17]

This kind of attitude – understandable though it may have been – could not, in the long run, help to further widespread democratic sentiments. It only strengthened the basic assumptions of Prussian state-consciousness, i.e. that all important decisions lay with the lofty heights of the state, and not with the lowlands of society. In everyday language, this meant 'politics for the people, not by the people'. It was Bismarck who, in the nineteenth century, did most to foster this attitude by putting it into political practice. Having made it quite obvious that he had no intention of letting matters take their own course, he proceeded to thrust himself, in the most Prussian of ways, into the limelight of current political developments. In a speech given on December 3 1850, one which he deemed worthy of quotation in his *Reflections and Reminiscences*, he commented: 'To me, Prussia's honour lies, above all, in the fact that it has eschewed all shameful association with democracy . . .'[18] Several years later, in a memorandum to the Prince of Prussia, he elaborated on this idea:

Prussia has become great not because of Liberalism and free-thinking, but because of a series of strong, decisive and wise Regents whose hands so carefully nurtured and spared the State's military and financial resources. At the same time, however, the Princes were autocratic enough to hold these resources ready, to be thrown unhesitatingly into the balance of European politics, should the right opportunity arise. And this is the system which we must retain if the monarchy is to survive for long. Parliamentary Liberalism may serve as a temporary means to an end, but it must never become that end itself.[19]

This was an almost classical expression of Prussia's course through the nineteenth century, a century dominated by the revolution in France. Parliamentarianism and democracy were not principles which accorded with the fundamental nature of the Prussian state; like any forces deriving from popular movements, they were ultimately of only instrumental – and therefore limited – usefulness. What was important was that the Prussian state could keep pace with modern political developments, not being outstripped by them but, on the contrary, actually striving to influence them itself. In this respect,

Prussia's path through the nineteenth century was not, in the widest sense, a restorative one. The state did not attempt, as did Austria, for instance, to by-pass contemporary trends, but instead absorbed them all: nationalism; industrialisation and the demands of the labour movement. This it did by subjecting them all to one single law: 'Modernity, yes; Democracy, no.'

It is not difficult to appreciate that this Prussian equation no longer worked out as straightforwardly as once it had done centuries before. Under Frederick the Great, the state had appeared to be a relatively convincing alternative to the *ancien régime* Estates. Similarly, Hardenberg and Stein's programme of social reform had helped Prussia to improve its image in comparison with revolutionary France. Under Bismarck, however, the state went too far: in wanting to exploit the industrial boom for its own political purposes, it gradually ended up itself serving the interests of industry and finance; in wanting to cripple the labour movement, its policy ultimately served only to strengthen the latter.[20]

Thus, for the first time ever, the Prussian concept of social control via the modernisation of the state was coming up against some tangible obstacles. It had indeed succeeded in curtailing democracy, but certain side-effects were making themselves apparent in a different guise. Virulent nationalism was gradually outgrowing the Prussian state's narrow frame of reference, offering broad sections of the populace something previously denied to them under Bismarck's undemocratic constitutional constructions. Similarly, the economic repercussions of an emergent mass society were disturbing to a state that was geared towards its predominantly agrarian provinces in the east. A new and uncontrolled set of dynamics had come into play. Last but not least, the labour movement was being driven away from its original position within the state; in order to match a masterful state, labour was finding it necessary to organise itself into a corpus of extremely large numbers.[21]

Developments such as these had left in their wake little of the Old Prussia. On the one hand, Prussia remained a partially-backward, particularist state of unprofitable rural provinces in the east, increasingly archaic and redundant. On the other hand, this was precisely why it continued to make far more of its characteristics as an authoritarian state than was actually good for the new *Reich* and its inhabitants. Hence, after the *Reich* was founded, Prussia's fondness for projecting an image of itself as tied by rattling chains of bondage to its army, an image which at times verged on becoming a self-caricature. This found tragi-comical expression in the story of the Captain of Köpenick, who achieved all that he desired by masquerading as a soldier. In Zuckmayer's play of the same name, an adaptation of a true story, a bitter dialogue on this subject takes place between Wilhelm Voigt (the phoney Captain of Köpenick) and his brother-in-law. The latter says: 'You're only a human being if you fit in with the human order. Even an insect is alive.' Voigt replies: 'Quite so! It is alive, Frederick! And do you know why it is alive? First there is the insect, and then there's the insect order! First there's the human, Frederick, and then the human order!.'[22]

This, then, was the impression given by Prussia at the time of its absorption into Germany: a state which judged its people according to their uniform, above all else. Fortunately, though, that was not all. During the period of the Weimar Republic, after the Hohenzollerns had already abdicated, Prussia re-emerged from the shadow of political reaction to play, unseen, a role which, a few years earlier, no-one would have believed possible: bastion of German democracy. Whilst *Reich* govern-ments came and went, victims of the vicissitudes of the period, the Prussian state government, led by the Social Democrat Prime Minister, Otto Braun, was a source of considerable political stability. It remained in office for over twelve years, and defended democracy – the same democracy which had once undergone so difficult a time in Prussia.[23] Ultimately, however, nothing could prevent Prussia from following the rest of the *Reich*, even though so many bearers of Prussian names were later to wage a resistance battle against Hitler. Prussia's time was up, its forces spent. Those who persist in mourning Prussia's passing would therefore do well to take note of this fact and devote themselves to other activities.

5 ✦ *PRUSSIA: how German was it?*

If, after the Second World War, demands were made that the Prussian question be re-examined, this very often stemmed from a desire – overt or covert – to end the territorial division of Germany. A century earlier, Prussia had shown Germany the way out of fragmentation, and the revival of Prussian traditions could again help to re-establish German unity, or so it was believed. The foremost proponent of this argument, the Erlangen historian Schoeps, repeatedly emphasised that 'there is indeed a Prussian Question which will become topical by the time Germany is re-unified, at the very latest.'[1] His ambitions for Prussia were made plain on a further occasion: 'The absence of Prussia means that today, the east and the west of Germany are detached from each other; this State can no longer fulfill its European function which was to bracket together, to bridge both east and west.'[2]

This statement, again with implications of Prussia's special role in unifying Germany, is based on the overhasty assumption that Prussia and Germany had been thrown upon one another by history and had done each other more good than harm overall. From this angle, Germany's unification would appear somewhat insipid without Prussian statehood, and Germany itself would seem dull and lacking in a core.[3] Yet we are forced – and not only by the unfortunate end to Prussian-German history in 1945 – to question whether there could be sufficient grounds for making this kind of assumption. Were historical relations between Prussia and Germany so harmonious as to prompt nothing more than regret at Prussia's disappearance?

An examination of actual events during past centuries at least urges some caution in passing judgement, and even offers some highly conflicting impressions.

To begin with, it should again be stressed that this is a question deriving from far deeper strata of history than is suggested by any nineteenth or twentieth-century disputes over unity and division. It is no coincidence that Heinrich von Treitschke – historian of the Prussian solution to Germany's problem during the Bismarck era – opens his extensive *History of Nineteenth Century Germany* with the Thirty Years War.[4] It is equally reasonable for the somewhat younger and more militant historian of the German Labour movement, Franz Mehring, to claim that Prussia's leadership of Germany (based on what he terms the 'Lessing-Legend') started during the reign of Frederick the Great.[5] Both historians regard the subject as inseparable from the problems which existed prior to the creation of the nation-state; both know well that any understanding of Prussia's position within Germany requires some consideration of its prehistory.

Treitschke's view of this prehistory is a straightforward one: 'From the midst of a chaotic mess of decayed measures of Imperial reform and incomplete territories, there arose the new Prussian State.'[6] In his opinion, the old *Reich* had shown that it was no longer viable; ever since the end of the Thirty Years War, at the latest, it had forfeited its claim to be a stabilising factor within the heart of Europe. Incapable of reforming itself, it also seemed unable to stimulate any kind of progressive improvement of social, political and economic conditions in Germany. In terms of constitutional law, above all, the *Reich* was a 'monster', as Pufendorf put it.

Indeed, Prussia's ascent is most intimately connected with the *Reich's* decline. Although today, with our enhanced knowledge of late-imperial history during the Age of Absolutism, we may no longer be quite so harsh in condemning the old *Reich's* limited scope for development,[7] little doubt remains that Prussia's power was amassed in an unequivocal departure from the imperial order. The acquisition of the crown by a *Land* not actually part of the *Reich* – the Duchy of Prussia – is just one expression of this emancipatory drive.

As the driving force behind the new German *Reich's* foundation in 1871, the Prussian state thus co-existed extremely uneasily with it. There was not a great deal of love lost between the two: Prussia cultivated its own image in sharp distinction to the claims put forward by the *Reich*; since the days of Frederick the Great, prayers for the *Kaiser* were no longer said in Prussian churches, and the victory at Rossbach over the '*Reich* Army, Croatian troops (pandours) and the French' gave a new boost to the self-confidence of the ambitious state.[8]

This tension between the ascendant Prussia and the obsolescent *Reich* is also identified by Franz Mehring, although he adopts a completely different approach. Unlike other socialist commentators, such as Lassalle,[9] however, Mehring does not argue that Frederick the Great destroyed the fossilised system of the old Empire with his 'revolutionary' decisions. He instead refers to a 'historical development going back over centuries'.[10] Mehring, too, is unable to find any evidence that the *Reich* freed itself from its mediaeval structures.

Not until the French Revolution and the Wars of Liberation was there any fresh impetus towards rapprochement between Prussia and the *Reich*. Both were suddenly thrown upon each other by the dynamism of events and new forces; neither one of them could escape the challenge of the new age. Whereas the *Reich* collapsed under the force of Napoleon's attack, surrendering its political existence, the state of Prussia survived, albeit weaker and diminished. It realised now that it was time to reinforce its hitherto state- and military-dominated existence, with the aid of national and domestic policies, and to abandon its self-imposed detachment *vis-à-vis* the German nation.

These ideas found very clear expression in the reform proposals advanced by several leading statesmen during the years of struggle against Napoleonic rule. Their aim was the revitalisation of the Prussian state, using national resources, although it soon became apparent that there were certain significant differences of interpretation. To the trained civil-servant Hardenberg, Prussian *raison d'état* remained a determining factor: the monarchy was to be strengthened by integrating as many social forces as possible into its institutions. To the *Reichsbaron* Stein from the west of Germany, Prussia's renewal constituted just part of the overall regeneration of Germany which he was hoping to witness; it was to serve the ascent of the nation as a whole. 'I have only one fatherland', he wrote on the eve of the Wars of Liberation, 'and that is Germany . . . At such a time, a time of momentous developments, I care not in the slightest about the dynasties.'[11]

By far the boldest plans for Prussia were those drawn up by Gneisenau, who saw an opportunity to harness the forces of nationalistic, anti-French sentiment for his own campaign for broader popular participation in domestic politics. He envisaged a Prussia which would lead the way for the whole of Germany in its constitutional development, thus becoming the most natural centre for the movement for national renewal. Writing from Paris in 1814, he emphasised that 'if a satisfactory constitution for the recently renewed and expanded Prussian monarchy is soon drawn up and proclaimed by the King, it will be the best possible bond between the newly-acquired territories and the old states; the other German states will start to draw comparisons between our system and theirs, awakening the desire for union with us'.[12]

Undoubtedly, these thoughts were well-justified in themselves; they also tied in with hopes that were held throughout Germany. On balance, though, they underestimated the inbuilt reservations underlying Prussia's aspirations with regard to its comparatively weak position *vis à vis* the other great powers. Such reservations increased particularly in light of the policies of restoration being pursued by Metternich's Austria. Prussia regarded itself not just as a German federal state, but also as a European great power with more than simply German interests to look after. Despite all the new national impulses, Prussian politics were not taken up exclusively with German issues.[13]

Prussia thus distanced itself somewhat from the German Confederation to which some of its provinces belonged, i.e. East and West Prussia, and Posen. It was a stance reflecting the emotional and political distance that history had placed between the two. Many East Elbians experienced this in their contact with Germans from the south or the west. The latter, in turn, were wary of forming too close an association with Prussia, even though they were waging a common struggle against the French. For instance, the Prussian traditionalist and opponent of Hardenberg's reform policies, Frederick August Ludwig von der Marwitz, wrote to the State Chancellor in September 1814: 'We are generally well-thought of as the liberators of the Teutonic fatherland, we are even loved for this in some places. Nevertheless, as Prussians, we are thoroughly despised. A virulent prejudice against this name prevails. Prussia seems utterly alien to all Germans. You only have to mention union with Prussia and everyone starts back in horror.'[14]

Marwitz accounts for this antipathy in terms of Prussia's 'old sins', which public opinion evidently ranked on a par with the 'recent atrocities perpetrated by the French'. Distrust was said to be so strong that 'the prospect of union with Prussia is almost as frightful as that of union with France'. At the same time however, 'the idea of a common German fatherland' had taken root so deeply that a Prussian policy for Germany without annexation seemed distinctly possible.[15]

Although both were affected by the National movement, it was not an easy task to bring Prussia and Germany to an agreement. No sooner had the Napoleonic threat to Europe been averted, than their particular interests were driven wide apart once more by their different historical experiences and political expectations. This was especially apparent in the matter of the constitution. Whereas the south German states were the least hesitant about embarking upon a path towards constitutional monarchy, Prussia performed a *volte face*, interrupting its development into a modern constitutional state, and abandoning plans to establish a representative body for the entire state.[16] In so doing, it once again appeared – to its fellow-German states – to embody an extreme form of monarchical absolutism, even though its reforms in areas such as municipal autonomy, agriculture and the army had just started to improve its overall image.

Had events taken a different turn, however, relations between Prussia and Germany would not, presumably, have become as harmonious as many nationalist writers hoped. Had Prussia pursued Gneisenau's plan and agreed to authentic popular representation, it would indeed have been in the forefront of constitutional progress throughout Germany. At the same time, though, this would have placed fresh obstacles in the path of a unified state. A Prussia with a fully-fledged system of popular representation would have been perfectly satisfied with itself and would have had even less desire to be incorporated into the rest of Germany. As paradoxical as it may sound: A semi-absolutist Prussia without any popular representation was undoubtedly deprived of an important channel of domestic integration. Yet precisely because of this, it remained particularly receptive towards the idea of German national consolidation.

Someone who had clearly recognised this fact was the Swabian Liberal, Paul Pfizer. In his *Correspondence Between Two Germans*[17] – published in 1831, a year after the July Revolution in France – he wrote:

Precisely because I consider a strong federative State constitution to be the ideal type suitable for our innate heterogeneity, I would almost hope – in Germany's interests – that the Prussian monarchy grants not general popular representation, but instead, freedom of the press and provincial assemblies, which would be worth a good deal more to us than this hollow pretence. If the introduction of general assemblies entails the complete centralisation of the present monarchy, this could easily mean that – instead of having a prepondering dynasty that conceals its unity in plurality – Germany would be dominated by the over-mighty Prussian race: A situation from which God, in his mercy, will hopefully spare us!![18]

As a south German, Pfizer thus feared that excessive development of the Prussian state – with a representative chamber encompassing Saarbrücken and Memel – would hinder Prussia's eventual amalgamation with Germany. This idea was expressed by Friedrich Meinecke in his work *Cosmopolitanism and*

the National State: 'The rest of Germany thenceforth had to take
into account not only the political wishes of the Prussian dynasty
but also those of the Prussian nation. This was bound to impede
considerably Prussia's national union with the rest of
Germany.'[19]

No matter how one looked at it, Prussia and Germany were
perpetually at cross-purposes with one another: if Prussia were
to develop into a fully constitutional state with its own body of
representatives, this would diminish interest in a German
national body of representatives. The latter would in any case
have appeared to be nothing more than a pale imitation of the
Prussian example. If, alternatively, Prussia were to remain a
semi-absolutist state lacking both a constitution and representation, this would have been a deterrent to the more progressive
German states, thus widening still further the gap that existed
between liberal non-Prussian Germany and conservative separatist Prussia.

This dilemma was notably apparent during the political
upheavals that shook nineteenth-century Germany during the
fateful era of the 1848 Revolution. Preceded by the series of
discussions on Prussia's future, in which tremendous expectations were placed on Frederick William IV, they also revealed
all the obstacles preventing any change from being made to
German affairs in the interests of the Hohenzollern state. It was a
matter of Germany advancing towards greater freedom and
unity: the question was whether Prussia represented more of a
help or a hindrance in this endeavour.[20]

These matters came in for much discussion during a debate
that sprang up, during the early 1840s, between Prussia and
non-Prussian Germany. It was first sparked off by the pen of an
East Elbian writer of considerable renown. In his *Prussia, Its
Constitution, Its Administration and its Relationship to Germany*, von
Bülow-Cummerow had been anxious to arouse sympathy for
Prussia's claim to superiority over Germany, without actually
mentioning any of the constitutional developments hoped for by
the Liberals. The main thrust of his argument ran as follows:
'We expect the rest of Germany to align itself with the greatest

purely-German power, namely Prussia.' The latter 'forms a shield against the giant of the east; it is Germany's forward defence against attack from the west. Its strength and concentration more than compensate for divided Germany's weakness'.[21]

It was, above all, power politics which lay behind Bülow-Cummerow's recommendation of Prussia to the Germans. He saw no need, however, to develop Prussia, along Liberal lines, into a fully-constitutional state, even though it was in sore need of reform and even though this would undoubtedly have made it domestically more attractive to the west and south of Germany. In its existing social and political form, Prussia was in his view the natural heart of a future Germany, 'appointed by Fate to set the world an example of how a monarchy must be if it is to have complete power to unite within itself the entire strength of the nation, whilst still granting a sufficient degree of freedom to its subjects'.[22]

These suggestions – although in many respects not unlike those later expressed by Bismarck – fell largely on deaf ears in non-Prussian Germany. A writer from Brunswick, Karl Steinacker, directly countered Bülow-Cummerow by pointing out that Prussia's existing constitution provoked extremely mixed reactions in other federal states of Germany, and that Prussia could not expect its claim to superiority to remain completely unchallenged. On the one hand, 'there is generally widespread belief that Germany's fate is inextricably linked to that of Prussia, and that to force the separation of their interests would spell disaster for them both'. On the other hand, however, 'there has always been a somewhat cold and hostile atmosphere between Prussia and Germany, which has prevented their close association and – to put it mildly – which has been all too obvious on certain occasions'.[23]

Steinacker attributed Germany's alienation from Prussia primarily to 'the way in which that originally small state had established its subsequent significance and stature'. 'Prussia had always gone its own separate way, eschewing common interests with Germany in favour of private ones. It is precisely this sort of militant ambition which did most to cause the body of the *Reich* to dissolve'. After the French Revolution, Prussia again opted for a 'separatist' course, only turning once more to Germany when obliged to do so by defeat: 'The year 1813 was the first time that Prussia publicly and solemnly declared its support for Germany.'[24]

What irritated the author most, however, was not so much Prussia's remoter past, as what he regarded as a more recent relapse into non-German traditions. He was anxious lest Prussia's interests as a European great power might cause it to lose sight of Germany. Above all, he was worried by the growth of political interest in Russia, which caused Prussia – unlike the rest of Germany – to mount permanent opposition to Poland.[25] From this angle, there was some threat of a separate 'Prussian nationality' developing, with a variety of consequences, even the emergence of a separate Prussian national consciousness. The 'separatist spirit, this tendency towards an outstanding Prussian state' was, in Steinacker's view, detrimental to the concept of the fatherland as a whole, a concept which was now coming to denote Prussia only.[26]

It was against a background of this kind of debate that Prussia and Germany entered the epoch of revolutionary change, ushered in by the year 1848. Faced with the same demand for greater freedom and unity, they had also to decide where to initiate the renewal of Central Europe. This was not simply a question of choosing between Berlin or Vienna; it was a decision as to whether the future political order was to be *kleindeutsch* or *grossdeutsch*, i.e. to exclude Austria, or to include the parts of Germany owned by the Habsburg monarchy. Equally, if not more so, it was a choice between Berlin and Frankfurt, i.e. a Prussian-dominated Germany, or a 'germanised' Prussia. There were not, as yet, any plans for only *Kleindeutschland*. Prussia's initial response to the critical 'March days' of 1848 was a somewhat confused acceptance of the second option. Events in Berlin prompted a shocked Frederick William IV to turn 'to my people and to the German nation', issuing the following address: 'I have today adopted the old German colours, and have placed myself and my people under the venerable banner of the German *Reich*. Prussia is henceforth merged into Germany.'[27] What this was actually supposed to entail was not elaborated upon, but a procedural suggestion was put forward: Germany's princes and parliaments were to be given the opportunity to convene with 'organs' of Prussia's existing United Diet as a 'Communal Assembly'. A resultant 'German Estates Assembly' was 'to debate the renaissance and establishment of a new, united and multiform Germany'.[28]

Nothing came of this proclamation, however, on account of the anticipated decision as to where the German Assembly was to be located. If the proposed consultative body was simply a committee assembly of the Prussian United Diet, enlarged to accommodate delegates from German provincial diets, then Berlin was to be the venue. Subjected to opposition from the south and west German states, though, this plan remained stillborn. Instead, within weeks, elections were held for rival national assemblies: a national German one in Frankfurt, a Prussian one in Berlin, and various constituent assemblies or revised provincial diets in other German capital cities.[29] Original hopes for uniform German constitutionalism had thus proved illusory. Despite considerable willingness on the part of the individual German states – Prussia included – to seek closer association with each other, and for the Hohenzollern state to be merged with Germany, even,[30] Prussia had ended up pursuing its own course of development after all, particularly as far as its constitution was concerned.

Upon critical reflection, one could say that Prussia was prepared to merge with Germany only in its moment of greatest need, during the first onslaught of the revolution. As soon as it had steadied itself once more, it reverted to an even stronger belief in its own strength. One should not, however, underestimate the 'German' orientation of Prussia's liberal middle classes, in particular. Its urban, educated and professional classes were predominantly German in their reactions to 1848, prepared to sacrifice the unity of the Hohenzollern state to the loftier cause of German unity.

Even Theodor Fontane – who later became Prussia's most renowned writer – at this time advocated that Prussia be dissolved and its provinces be directly integrated into a national German fatherland. 'Germany's resurrection', he wrote, in an article entitled 'Prussia's Future',[31] 'will entail many heavy sacrifices. Of these, the greatest will be made by Prussia. Prussia is to die. Every other state can and may be merged into Germany, but Prussia has to be submerged.' He concluded: 'Prussia has only two options: to sink without trace into Germany, or to shrink to its original territory of 1740. There can be no doubt as to which of the two options is the more attractive – to die thus or to live as described.'[32]

Another subsequent advocate of the Prussian cause, the Pomeranian historian Johann Gustav Droysen, also chose, at this stage of the revolution, to argue vehemently in favour of Prussia's dissolution.[33] In a memorandum, dated 29 April 1848, to the like-minded Prussian Foreign Minister, Heinrich von Arnim, he warned against developing Prussia into a fully-constitutional state. His advice was to let Germany make the first political move:

Prussia shall 'merge' into Germany; that is, instead of maintaining a separate constitutional identity, it will, by developing a provincial Estates-oriented constitution, be able to strengthen its ties with both Germany and the individual states, so as to offer its own mighty and efficient organisations – military and financial, above all – as a suitable pattern for the nation as a whole.[34]

In case the policy of Prussian dissolution should fail, Droysen was contemplating a further option not unlike his subsequent prussocentric ideas: Prussia was to acquire a full constitution so that it could become the focal point of the new Germany. 'If there is a breakdown in the current reorganisation of Germany', he wrote, shortly before the event, 'then Prussia's constitution must be absolutely watertight and must become the central land of the new Empire, to which any land wishing to be German may attach itself.'[35]

The political events of 1848 took a more rapid turn than Droysen had anticipated. The war with Denmark over

Schleswig-Holstein revealed how greatly the Frankfurt National Assembly depended upon Prussian aid; without the Prussian Army, there was no possible way of effecting federal policy decisions. Yet when the Berlin National Assembly turned out to be more radical than its Frankfurt counterpart, Prussia regained its focal importance for a new reason: left-wing elements, too, were now starting to favour Berlin once more.[36]

It was precisely this development which caused Prussia a – temporary – setback and allowed the Germans in Frankfurt to make up some of the ground they had lost. The radicalism of the Berlin National Assembly prompted the Prussian government to banish it to Brandenburg. Suddenly, it seemed as though the Frankfurt Assembly could rid itself of a troublesome rival and also revive original plans for a single, supra-regional German parliament, senior to a number of regional parliaments more or less equal to one another in importance. The Assembly's President, Heinrich von Gagern, himself travelled to Berlin in order to persuade the Prussian King that this was a unique opportunity to solve the 'Prussia/Germany' problem. To Frederick William IV, the possibility of being *Kaiser* of Germany without having to develop Prussia into a constitutional *Grosstaat* seemed, for a moment, to be a unique opportunity.[37]

But, being less accommodating now than he had been during the early days of the March Revolution, he turned down the idea. In the meantime, however, the forces of pro-Prussian patriotism had rallied too strongly to be restrained by any calls for self-discipline. Instead, the King resolved the problem of revolution in a classically Prussian manner: he dissolved the National Assembly and imposed a constitution. Surprisingly liberal, had this not been tainted by being a Royal decree, rather than a resolution passed by the Constituent Assembly, it would have been comparable with other German constitutions of the period.

The new constitution, proclaimed on 5 December 1848 and referred to always as the 'Imposed Constitution' (*Oktroyierte Verfassung*), marked a milestone in Prussian–German history.[38] It signalled that Prussia had found its feet once again as a state and was now fully determined to continue making its distinctive mark upon history. This was not unlike the traditional pattern of official policy in the Prussian state. Certain limited allowances were made for the passing of time. Various changes in the political landscapes were taken into account; the consequences of the French Revolution were accepted but at no point were the motivating factors or impulses allowed to come to the fore.

Prussia did not meet the challenge of the revolution with purely counter-revolutionary measures, as Austria was so keen to do. It did not simply dismiss out of hand the nationalist movement or the demands made by the constitutionalists. But it was not prepared to abandon the principle of state control over social developments, nor would it see its jurisdiction eroded by a process of national self-realisation. It was with this aim in mind that a conservative deputy in the newly-elected Second Chamber of the Prussian parliament, Otto von Bismarck, became passionately committed to greater Prussian autonomy: 'The Frankfurt Crown may glisten greatly, but the gold that lends truth to its shine can only be gained by melting down the Prussian Crown, and I very much doubt that this constitution will be the right mould for such a re-casting operation.'[39]

In order to understand the newly-awakening Prussian self-assurance that was expressed by Bismarck, mention must be made not only of the difficulties faced by the German National Assembly in Frankfurt, but also of the fierce loyalty to the Hohenzollern dynasty that – rekindled by the crisis of authority in 1848 – became particularly virulent in rural areas and in the ranks of both the army and officialdom. In the case of Bismarck, it was undoubtedly his awareness of the old-Prussian dynasty which led him to declare, in a speech to the Chamber in 1849:

What has kept us going has been nothing other than pure Prussianism. It was the vestiges of our much-censured, out-and-out Prussianism which survived the revolution: the Prussian army, the Prussian heritage, the fruit of years of intelligent Prussian administration and the vital inter-relationship between the King and his subjects. It was the faithfulness of the Prussian populace to their ancestral dynasty, it was the old Prussian virtues of honour, loyalty, obedience and the courage found throughout the army, from the officer corps right down to the rawest recruits . . .[40]

Bismarck's defiant eulogy of an old Prussia in the style of Frederick was noticeably derogatory in tone about the rest of Germany. It was directed not so much towards an internal, as towards an external threat to Prussia: its depersonalisation by the *Reich*. Traumatic fears of a return to old dependencies upon the latter reverberate throughout this eulogy:

The people who created and who are most truly represented by the army do not need to see their Prussian kingdom fading into the rotting morass of South German confusion. The people are bound, in their loyalty, not to a paper ruler of the *Reich*, but to the living and autonomous King of Prussia, his ancestors' true heir . . . We all wish the Prussian eagle to spread its wings over our land, protecting and governing us, from the Memel to the Donnersberg. It must remain free, however, and not be fettered by a new *Reichstag* in Regensburg, with its wings unscathed by those egalitarian hedgeclippers from Frankfurt . . .[41]

In fact, fears about Prussia's possible bondage were to play a prominent role during the ten years following the revolution. As events turned out, it was not the Germany of the *Paulskirche* but, instead, the revived German Confederation under Austrian leadership that kept Prussia in a position of dependence. It was not the new Frankfurt Assembly, but the old Frankfurt *Bundestag* which was soon to revive memories of the Regensburg *Reichstag*, where Prussia felt so shabbily treated. But the decision had been made: Since Prussia had eschewed association with liberal Germany of the *Paulskirche*, it soon fell into the arms of the old powers against which it had scarcely any forces of resistance. Prussia capitulated to Austrian demands for an end to all Union of Princes policies, in a convention signed at Olmütz in December 1850. The 'Olmütz Disgrace' came to symbolise Prussia's lack of independence and of sovereignty.[42]

This dilemma in which Prussia found itself continued to reverberate throughout the 1850s. It was clear that the nationalist movement made the situation still more difficult as Prussia was no longer able – as once it had been, during the eighteenth century – to vent its wrath upon the *Reich* by retreating into isolation. Withdrawal from the Frankfurt parliament was now no longer sufficient. This view was expressed particularly eloquently by the philosopher Paul de Lagarde, a supporter of the nationalist cause. In an impassioned essay of 1853, entitled 'Conservative', he wrote:

Prussia was created out of necessity. It can only survive by driving itself beyond its own limits; it must keep going if it is to avoid the humiliation of falling. It must move onwards because it has come too far to turn back now. Prussia is a hiker who, having achieved three-quarters of the ascent, dare not stop to admire the view, but must push on to the summit.[43]

Prussia set about this ascent aided not by attempts at constitutional policies, but by economic and trade policy achievements. During the years of political reaction following Olmütz, the industrialisation process was accelerating, particularly in Prussia's western provinces. Furthermore, thanks to the continued existence of the German Customs Union, economic relations between the non-Austrian states of Germany were growing ever-closer. There was also the development of the railway network forcing Prussia out of its isolation. The major lines running from Berlin to the east, south, west and north helped considerably to link Prussian and non-Prussian areas of Germany.[44]

Nevertheless, the most crucial incentive towards improved Prussian/German relations came, ultimately, from various shifts in the balance of power outside Germany. After the Crimean War, the conservative great powers saw their position weakened, there was an upsurge of the Italian national movement during the war against Austria, and both factors meant that by the early sixties, the political map of Europe had undergone considerable change within a ten-year period. It was now becoming apparent in Germany, too, that issues raised by the 1848 Revolution had been just temporarily shelved and still needed to be settled. If they remained unsettled, they were likely to constitute a real threat to peace.

Swayed by this consideration, Bismarck – at this time still serving as Prussia's envoy to St Petersburg – composed his important Baden-Baden memorandum for the new King of Prussia, William I. Warning against the dangers of postponing the national question still further, he offered an assessment of the situation:

The entire German population is nursing increasing disgruntlement that a great and powerful nation should be forced, on account of its constitutional shortcomings, to forego its rightful influence in Europe. Furthermore, it has to live in constant fear of attack by neighbours who, in different circumstances, would pose no threat whatsoever. The more widespread this feeling becomes, the greater the danger to every German government.[45]

Bismarck was convinced that Germany was in desperate need of reform. Without abandoning the Prussian stance he had held at the time of the 1848 Revolution, his experiences as Prussian envoy to the Frankfurt Federal Diet now told him how urgent the German question had become. Accordingly, he suggested the establishment of 'a national body to represent the German people at the Federal central authority', with members to be elected by the individual German provincial diets. Admittedly, this was only an embryonic form of the later German *Reichstag* directly elected by the people, but certain basic principles for subsequent policy during the unification period were already contained here in outline – national representation, not for its own sake as an idealistic expression of the nation's self-realisation, but instead with a certain prescribed value within the context of an intricate power structure. It was intended to 'counteract' any 'tendencies towards individualistic dynastic policies' and to redress an imbalance of majorities in the Federal Diet. Bismarck refers almost casually to a further point of significance: that the proposed national representation would also 'lessen the substantial load of domestic policy issues borne by the Prussian government *vis à vis* the electorate and the Chambers'.[46] In other words, far from trying to express the old 1848 problem of rival bodies of popular representation in Frankfurt and Berlin, he wished to give it a novel twist. If one of them were to cause trouble, the other would provide a useful alternative means of exercising power. *Divide et impera* would have been a fitting motto for defining the Prussian/German balance of power.[47]

The fulfilment of German-national aspirations was to be an important factor during the subsequent years of political manoeuvres towards the founding of the *Reich*. Twelve months after the Baden-Baden memorandum, Bismarck was appointed Prime Minister of Prussia and was immediately confronted with a situation requiring national forces to be strengthened, not solely for external reasons. Opening up possibilities of solving the German question was the fastest way to strike a blow against the Liberals – with their parliamentary majority – during the conflict surrounding the reform of Prussia's army. Given a dichotomy between national and liberal ambitions, the Liberals – as the main protagonists of the national movement – were thus forced into an extremely awkward position.[48]

With regard to the constitutional problems entailed in the imminent shake-up within central Europe, this meant that the parliamentary principle was accepted, subject to certain narrow restrictions, as a structural element of the Prussian/German balance of power. Bismarck's plan did not allow a Prussian or a German parliament to occupy a key position in balancing German domestic interests, and neither parliament was to take it upon itself to introduce a new political order. He had no intention of even allowing Prussia to become a fully-parliamentary state, with Germany following in its wake as an acceptable alternative to the 1848 concept of Germany's complete parliamentary development. Neither solution seemed, in his view, to take sufficient account of certain historical realities. What he was seeking, however, was a solution which – by combining several complementary institutions, including parliament – could strengthen the King of Prussia's position. Having successfully founded the North German Federation and excluded Austria, he commented, in retrospect: 'The manner in which the King reigns over Germany has never seemed especially important to me; what has been my concern – to the very best of my God-given powers – is the fact that he *does* reign at all.'[49]

The emphasis given, in the proposals for political reform, to the power of the Prussian King and of the government, was to have a very ambivalent effect upon Prussian/German relations. On the one hand, the restriction imposed upon parliamentary development blunted the edge of the rivalry that existed between the two parliaments. Prussia's parliament and that of North Germany (later to become the German *Reichstag*) were no longer as mutually competitive as the two national assemblies of 1848 in Berlin and Frankfurt – both spurred on by increasing desire for integration – had been. On the other hand, precisely this limited status of the two parliamentary institutions had the paradoxical result of firmly entrenching political backwardness in Prussia, the very state which Bismarck wished to strengthen. This was because the Prussian parliament was still elected on the basis of a three-class suffrage dating from the early period of reaction. The German *Reichstag* however – convened partly as a catalyst to national developments – was to attain much greater significance as the product of universal equal suffrage. In parliamentary terms, the foundation of the *Reich* ousted Prussia into second place.

This shift of significance between Prussia and Germany had not escaped the notice of critical observers at the time. Old-Prussian conservatives, especially, fell to predicting how the newly-created *Reich* would neither conserve nor promote Prussian interests, but instead detract from them. In contrast to other critics of the *Reich*, they foresaw the danger not of a *Grosspreussen*, a Prussianisation of Germany, but conversely, of an impairment of Prussia's individuality. Their anxieties were, of course, underpinned by quite concrete fears that their own economic and political interests would be eroded. Nevertheless, this did not alter the fact that they recognised more clearly than others how it was only at surface level that Bismarck's victories appeared to be Prussia's victories.[50]

The shift of emphasis away from Prussia towards Germany was especially apparent in the case of the Poles. Up until then, inhabitants of the territories acquired by Prussia during partition were allowed to hold Prussian citizenship only, irrespective of their nationality. Thereafter, they were obliged to adapt themselves to the national state of Germany, which was soon to threaten their own national development. Suspecting the likelihood of this occurring, Polish deputies protested, during one of the first sessions of the new German *Reichstag*, against proposals to transform Prussians into German nationals, stating: 'Gentlemen, it is our desire to remain, until God determines otherwise, under Prussian rule. We do not, however, wish to be incorporated into the German *Reich*.'[51] Within just a few years, this statement was justified. On 28 August 1876, it was decreed by law that 'the business of every authority, every public servant and every political body of the state' was thereafter to be conducted exclusively in German. Deliberate attempts were to be made to suppress the Polish language.[52]

The old pan-German critics of Bismarck's *Reich* also saw problems in this shift of emphasis, though from a different point of view. Apart from the exclusion of Austria, they also lamented, on the one hand, the 'unnatural' situation whereby 'the old western Germany that had its own history for centuries, long before there was even any question of there being a Prussia . . . is now being ruled by the latter'.[53] On the other hand, the author of this criticism, Constantin Frantz, was well aware of the opportunities open to non-Prussian Germans within the *Reich*, for elsewhere he stated:

Euphoric with military victories, Prussia not only deludes itself as to its ability to solve the German question, it also completely fails to recognise how its subsequent position in Germany – which represents, in its own view, an extraordinary increase in power – is actually undermining its very existence . . . No matter what issues forth from the *Reichstag*, it can no longer be specifically Prussian.[54]

This prediction was in fact totally accurate. With every year that elapsed, German interests gradually acquired more weight in the new *Reichstag*. Before long, it became necessary to enact a protective customs policy in order to safeguard the landowning *Junkers* – the bastion of Old Prussia – from financial ruin. If one can simply imagine for a moment: East Elbian Prussia, birthplace of none other than the very founder of the German Empire himself, being reduced to the role of the nation's country retreat, provincial and in need of protection! Friedrich Naumann had been right when recalling, in his bestselling book *Democracy and Empire*, how 'in 1866, the old conquering Prussia took one last big bite into the old German Empire before lying down to sleep. Prussia has stopped growing. William I was the last King of Prussia in the old sense'.[55]

Indeed, the concepts of rulership held by the last reigning Hohenzollerns are a clear illustration of how emphasis shifted away from Prussia towards the German Empire. Whilst William I had only reluctantly accepted the title of German *Kaiser* and always preferred to think of himself first and foremost as King of Prussia, Wiliam II saw himself as *Kaiser*, above all else. His contemporaries were well aware of this and thus spoke only of 'the *Kaiser*'. A great number of Prussia's enemies were encouraged by this trend, amongst them Constantin Frantz: 'As a result, the people of Prussia no longer know who is their true head – the King of Prussia, or the German *Kaiser*. The more they would like to favour the latter, the more they would cease to feel Prussian. And what else would that signify other than that Prussia is in the process of swallowing itself up?'[56]

Yet this was not quite so straightforward a process. Undoubtedly, Old Prussia had, to a certain extent, entered into a marriage in which the partner's family were to prove the stronger in the long term. Nevertheless, Prussia had in turn made its mark upon the family, in terms of the outward trappings of power and influence. Ranging from the army, which – despite its federal structure – was predominantly influenced by Prussia, to the social mores not dissimilar to the ideals of order prevalent in Prussian military and civil service, the new *Reich* was tinged by a certain ethos regarded universally as 'Prussian', even though Old-Prussians might not have recognised it as representative of their own particular character. As a social type, the reserve lieutenant wore Prussian colours.

In some ways, Prussia's embodiment within the phenomena of the army was consistent, even, for how else could the old Hohenzollern state have shown itself off to best advantage in the new German Empire? Thanks to Bismarck, the low status accorded to parliamentary institutions had caused civilian domains to lose a great deal of prestige. A parliament elected on a three-class suffrage had little claim to honour in a dynamically developing industrial society, and a functioning bureaucracy was not in itself enough to counteract the army's predominance. The civil servant was no match for the military officer.[57]

But it was not simply in the militarisation of society that the Bismarckian tie between Prussia and Germany was apparent.[58] It also emerged in the growth of anti-liberal tendencies within every sphere of social and political life. Given that the *Reich* had come into being as the product of military and power-related manoeuvrings, rather than through the democratic process, it had, from the very outset, never been sufficiently integrated politically. This particular type of deficit created a perpetual search for some kind of compensation. There was some anxiety that, after so much care and effort had been expended in its creation, the *Reich* might yet collapse. All those hesitating to fall in wholeheartedly with the new political order were roundly denounced as enemies of the *Reich*. There were fears also of disagreements over political alternatives and, accordingly, conflicts were repressed instead of being publicly aired. Again, for fear of a relapse into weakness and impotence, categories such as 'unity, solidarity and adaptability' were valued more highly than others such as 'freedom, tolerance and a plurality of opinion'.[59]

Admittedly, not all of these ominously anti-liberal phenomena can be attributed to Bismarck's union of Prussia with Germany. There are other important factors, most notably the rapid change of economic and social conditions resulting from industrialisation. This came at a time of struggle for domestic consolidation within the *Reich*, and served only to exacerbate the existing uncertainty. But without doubt, the *Reich's* inadequate integration – itself related to the troubled relations between Prussia and Germany – was one of the most important reasons why potentially controversial issues came to be suppressed. In consequence, the political climate grew increasingly illiberal. The general tendency for all disagreements to be swept under the carpet or else disguised can thus only be accounted for in the light of this specific shortcoming.

Historians of a nationalist persuasion have nearly all underestimated the severity of the problems of integrating a state which lacks social, ethnic and religious structural homegeneity. Borne up by their belief that people of one culture and one language naturally belong together, such historians have tended to overlook the distinctions arising from centuries of separation into discrete countries and territories. They have failed to recognise how important it is to have a fully-constitutional parliamentary system if precisely these kinds of distinction are to be ironed out.[60] Closer – but also harsher – judgement has been made, on the other hand, of how Prussian/German unification meant drawbacks for certain people. The socialists, above all, suffered particularly under illiberal rule although they nevertheless refused to be driven out of the *Reich* or to abandon their hopes of a future Prussian state. In his memoirs, published shortly before outbreak of the First World War, August Bebel weighed up the pro's and con's of Bismarck's creation:

Supposing, for a moment, that Prussia had lost in 1866, Bismarck's Ministry and the squirearchy of Junkers . . . would not have been swept away. No-one knew that better than Bismarck. The Austrian government would never have grown as strong after victory as the Prussian government. In its entire structure, the Austrian State was and is internally weak, completely unlike Prussia. However, the government of a strong State is a greater threat to its democratic development . . . If Austria had won, its government would in all probability have attempted to rule Germany by reaction. In so doing, it would have aroused the hostility of not only the entire Prussian population, but also the majority of Germans and a good number of Austrians. If ever a revolution had fair prospects of success, it was against Austria and at that particular time. The result would have been the democratic union of the *Reich*, something which Prussia's victory made impossible.[61]

Bebel's words express with unusual clarity how ambivalent the founding of the Prussian–German *Reich* was. It prevented a revolution, which in negative terms meant that politics were driven under the yoke of an authoritarian system. Viewed in positive terms, however, it did set the forces of Socialism on the path towards reformism. Conditions within the Prussian--German authoritarian state forced Social Democrats, in turn, to form themselves into a tightly-disciplined and strong party, one which could ill-afford any fragmentation or sectarianism. As a counterbalance to the mighty government, the Social

Democrats proved themselves to be equally united and rigorous.

As Bebel's party gained strength, the Prussian state reverted to its bulwark function: The more influence and votes acquired by the Social Democrats, the more Prussia harked back to its old role of countering every move towards parliamentary democracy in the *Reich*. In the last years before the First World War, as universal suffrage throughout the Empire was proving to be of distinct advantage to the Social Democrats and the *Reich* itself was building up its influence, the Chancellor of the *Reich* von Bethmann Hollweg felt it advisable, during a debate in the Prussian Upper Chamber, to enter an emphatic plea for the preservation of the Prussian kingdom's power structure and position. Answering those anxious to bring Prussian suffrage into line with that of the *Reich*, he stressed that:

Prussia will always and must always have a different domestic structure to that of the *Reich*. The latter's innovation, based on the broad masses, needs the Prussian state which was built upon the firm foundations of the army and the indissoluble community that binds the people and their ruling dynasty. This is the strong support required to face every vicissitude. This has been Prussia's historical vocation, and will remain so for decades to come. No Prussian statesman will ever be prepared to sacrifice this to the juggernaut of democratic tendencies.[62]

This was another unmistakeable example of Prussian *raison d'état*. There was no question here of Prussia having fulfilled its historical mission with the founding of the *Reich* in 1871. Instead, this was a clear reminder that Prussia had a central role to play in the new German Empire – that of counteracting burgeoning democracy. The '*rocher de bronze*' established by Frederick William I thus remained unscathed by the ins and outs of imperial politics. Bethmann Hollweg assessed the situation as follows: 'Prussia's presidial power was created not to represent Prussian particularism, but to bring to *Reich* affairs the full force of the concept of the State, which Prussia embodies.'[63]

Prussia was thus regarded here not merely as a geographical concept, as a Federal State much like any other, but as the actual embodiment of a state-concept[64] which had withstood the passing of time. This 'concept of the state' was devised in direct opposition to certain libertarian developments in the social sphere, and much depended upon whether and in what way it was challenged by society. At the time of the founding of the empire, the state-concept had been used to back up a policy which could be described as being a partly progressive, if authoritarian attempt to hack through the Gordian knot of the 1848 legacy. On the eve of the First World War, however, it was to act as a braking mechanism, in a reactionary attempt to slow down and halt, if at all possible, the growth of parliamentary democracy in the German *Reich*. Thereafter, Prussia was to be allocated the role not of engine but of brake. Consequently, it had less and less opportunity of actively influencing the way in which the *Reich* developed.

At the end of its monarchy period, Prussia was thus once more in a situation of conflict with the *Reich*. Whereas, during the seventeenth and eighteenth centuries, conflict had arisen as a result of Prussia's emancipatory departure from what it held to be a backward and impotent empire, this particular conflict had a retrogressive effect upon Prussia. Now, it was not the *Reich* but Prussia that was the 'stronghold of reaction' and stagnation. It required the events of 9 November 1918 to rescue the Hohenzollern state from its *cul de sac*.

It was by no means a straightforward road that was to lead Prussia, from the social and political constraints marking the monarchy's final stages, out into the world thrown open by the new republic. Under the novel circumstances ushered in by the start of Germany's democratic renewal, it became a matter of tremendous controversy as to whether the Prussian state was to continue to exist or whether – by taking advantage of the prevailing climate of upheaval – it was to be dissolved into component provinces. Broad majorities within the two Socialist parties, the MSPD (Majority Social Democrats) and the USPD (Independent Social Democrats), and within the pro-Republican parties of the 'bourgeois' camp – the left-liberal DDP (German Democratic Party) and the *Zentrum* (Catholic Centre Party) – initially favoured the dissolution or splitting of Prussia in order to clear the way for a better, more balanced structure of the new Germany. It was, above all, the liberal lecturer in Constitutional Law, Hugo Preuss – appointed State Secretary in the *Reich* Office of the Interior by the Council of People's Deputies – who did most towards ending Prussia's existence as state. In his draft for a new *Reich* constitution, he stated that to maintain a major state of 40,000,000 inhabitants inside a whole republic larger by only half as much again was 'a constitutional, political and economic impossibility'.[65]

The year 1919 brought discussions which were in many respects simply a rehash of those held during the 1848 Revolution. The forces striving for Germany's democratic renewal were, in the vast majority, dubious about the prospect of an equally constitutional Prussian Constituent Assembly working in parallel to the German National Assembly. Prophetically, a great number of those in favour of a united German state expressed concern that it would not be as easy or as defensible to dissolve a democratically-renewed Prussia as it would be to dissolve the politically-backward state left over from the imperial period.[66]

Counterforces, swift to rally, were confident that Prussia would indeed undergo this process of re-consolidation. Concentrated mainly in those southern German states most fearful for their own future, they also gained strength in areas to the north, west and east of Germany. Here, belief in an inner and an external threat to the *Reich* meant that many were all too willing to contravene outdated official regulations. This was true, above all, of Social Democrat leaders in the Prussian government who – despite their basic approval of policies aimed at greater unity for the *Reich* – still felt that it would be dangerous to do away with Prussia under those particular circumstances. This was why, at the opening of Prussia's *Landesversammlung* (Constituent Assembly), the new Prime Minister Paul Hirsch implored the deputies to concern themselves with the new Prussia:

The old Prussia has gone for good. A new Prussia is born . . . It is now up to you to give free Prussia a new and lasting official shape. From being one of the most politically backward states in the world, you have to turn it into the most libertarian and most progressive. You have to eliminate the foreign aversion to Prussia.[67]

Hirsch not only appealed for Prussia's democratic renewal, he also went on to discuss the new relationship between Prussia and Germany:

We are not interested in particularism. Prussia is perfectly willing to amalgamate with the *Reich* . . . but surely, breaking Prussia into inefficient and unviable miniature fragments would be the most unsuitable way imaginable to achieve a united German state. It would spell disaster for our economy, for communications and for our cultural activities as well. As long as the south German states . . . form independent member states, then Prussia, too, must remain a united constituent State. Progress towards German unity is not furthered by having a proliferation of individual states.[68]

There then followed the most important argument in favour of Prussia's – temporary – preservation:

A free Prussia is no longer the bogey of yesteryear from which one used to flee, fearful of its lethal dominance over Germany. It was only the old Prussia of Junkers and reaction that spelt danger for Germany. The new Prussia, that of liberty for all the people, will be a blessing to the entire German fatherland.[69]

The distinction between old and new Prussia was actually a – highly successful – attempt to take the wind out of the sails of what was seen as a foolish desire for Prussia to merge into a larger, still indeterminate *Reich* entity. In line with the old and trusted adage of a bird in the hand being worth two in the bush, the new Prussian government was attempting to safeguard what it had already achieved, though it did not give up all hope for certain other longer-term objectives. The German question, one might say, was thus left in abeyance.

This was particularly true of Hirsch's successor as Prime Minister, Otto Braun, politically the most able member of the Social Democratic party. With his profound understanding of how historical realities had evolved, he not only wanted to see every possible threat to the Prussian state removed, but also wished to see it strengthened, as the heart of a future united German Republic. Against the background of the Frankfurt *Paulskirche*'s shattered dreams of a united *Reich*, Bismarck had ultimately pursued a German policy centred on Prussia. Similarly, against the background of abortive attempts at renewal during the turbulent years of 1918/19, Braun strove to consolidate Prussia with the aim of helping Germany's future development. He emphatically rejected the idea that 'Prussia must die in order that the *Reich* may live', and his conviction that Prussia was a state with a democratic mission led him to demand that it become the focal point of a united German Republic:

> I am far more convinced that the strongest expression of unity today in Germany is provided by the great, self-contained and unitary structure of the Prussian State. This is why, if we wish to establish a solidly united German *Reich*, we must preserve the State of Prussia.[70]

Braun's stance was further influenced by party political factors, and he remained loyal to it throughout his period in office, lasting almost until the end of the Weimar Republic. It meant that greater *Reich* unity was to be sought not in the dismantling but, on the contrary, in the strengthening of Prussia, and that the old Hohenzollern state was intended to become something of a centre of democracy. Prussia's leadership role within Germany was now justified by the significance of its republican-democratic reorganisation.

Throughout the upheavals of the Weimar period, Prussia was indeed to serve as a democratic counterweight to a politically unbalanced Germany. Whereas *Reich* governments changed constantly and lost their parliamentary-democratic basis by 1930, Prussia demonstrated remarkable political continuity, which it was able to maintain right up to 1932. With only minor interruptions, Prussia was governed by 'Weimar Coalition' cabinets, consisting of Social Democrats, left-liberal Democrats and the Catholic Centre party. Despite their full support for the Republic, by 1920 these had lost all chances of forming a government in the *Reich*. It was not an exaggeration when Prussia was described as the 'bulwark' of democracy in the German Republic.[71]

This is certainly a favourable image of Prussia, compared to that projected in earlier years. To progress from being a 'stronghold of reaction' to become a 'stronghold of republicanism' is anything but straightforward! Upon closer examination, it is perhaps not all that astonishing, however. Underneath the backwardness of its constitutional structure, historical Prussia had actually brought about the breakthrough of a variety of modern forces that might otherwise never have emerged. A comparison with Habsburg Austria, the rival German power of the eighteenth and nineteenth centuries, is sufficient to reveal the chances made available to progressive forces in Prussia. No-one saw this more clearly than one of Imperial Germany's harshest critics: Walter Rathenau, a major industrialist of Jewish extraction, temporarily Foreign Secretary during the Weimar Republic. Shortly after the First World War, he published *The New State*, a discussion of the pro's and con's of preserving Prussia, whose historical individuality he particularly admired.

Prussia – once so greatly idolised, now so bitterly despised – is being destroyed in accordance with the maxim *quidquid delirant reges, plectuntur archivi*. Forgotten is the degree of organisational strength which Prussia brought to the *Reich*. Forgotten is the non-German force and clarity of will, the ability to carry something out and see it through to the finish, the tremendous economic might and the self-critical matter-of-factness. Compare the Holy Roman Empire and the German *Reich*: What do you have left? Prussia. Remove Prussia from Germany and what do you have left? The Confederation of the Rhine. An extended version of Austria. A clerical republic.[72]

What swayed Rathenau in Prussia's favour was not the appeal of Prussian discipline at a time of upheaval, nor was it the hope of a democratised Prussia proving attractive to the republican *Reich*. It was instead the knowledge that Prussia had a special historical characteristic which, in his view, was crucial to Germany's entire future development: the strength of Prussia's political structure. Notwithstanding the severe criticism – which he himself, among others, had voiced – of the repressive aspects of the Prussian monarchy,[73] he detected certain forces at work within Prussian history, without which Germany would have been much worse off. Germany without Prussia he likened to a cultural landscape harking back to medieval times, fearful of progress, politically flaccid and inert in the face of modern-day challenges. He did, however, regard Prussia as having failed in its mission to determine the inner shape of the German *Reich*: Germany continued to be an economic–military interest group of various dynasties'.[74] This did not lessen non-Prussian Germany's political deficit, which remained a 'soft core in the hard outer crust of Prussianism'.[75]

It was this lack of political fusion which caused Rathenau to remain preoccupied with the subject of Prussia, even after November 1918. Although he did not in the slightest let up in criticising the evils of the Old-Prussian military state, he did advise against too rash an abandonment of the political energies associated with Prussia. He painted a precise picture of what he feared would happen to Germany without Prussia:

By declaiming our guilty conscience, our feudal-militaristic conscience, Prussia's virtues have become hackneyed and debased. We dread constantly hearing the term 'categoric imperative' whenever the bureaucracy is meant, hearing about Old-Prussian simplicity whenever Junker privileges are being defended, and hearing that the monarchy is matter-of-fact when liberty is being stifled and the plebs are to be flung into gaol. And yet one thing is true, and remains so: political collectivism and national community – not to be confused with the simple love of one's native country, community with one's tribe and local interest – have never been found anywhere in Germany other than in, and through, Prussia.[76]

This was not Rathenau's last word on the subject of Prussia's historical individuality. He concluded his analysis with a final sentence which, unfortunately, has never been quoted: 'This is precisely because Prussia is just as un-German as it is German.'[77] If, according to Rathenau, Prussia amounted to something greater then a run-of-the-mill German Federal *Land*, greater than a mere tribal community, then this was not only because of its German elements, but also, in particular, because of its non-German approach. To Rathenau, Prussia was not an extension or sublimation of Germany – as the German Nationalists of his day wished it to be seen – but instead a historical reality of its own kind, shaped not just by Germany alone. He expressed this idea as follows: 'Prussia, which justly bore the name and the Crown of provinces outside Germany, appointed itself the task of uniting Germany as a State.' But, 'in spite of its position of leadership and its admirable unity, monarchic Prussia remained, spiritually and politically, a non-German entity, created for external, but not internal, conquest . . .'[78]

Rathenau had thus retained a certain sensitivity to the ambivalencies of Prussian *raison d'état*. More than other observers, he sensed the tensions and differences between Prussia and Germany, and like Bismarck before him, he still saw a supra-national dimension to the Prussian question.[79] There were still those, however, who refused to acknowledge this, dismissing all of Prussia's non-German elements as incompatible with *raison d'état*, or else banishing them from their political consciousness. These people were partly responsible for causing Prussia to lose both the justification for its existence and, eventually, that very existence itself. The German-National interpretation of history – according to which Prussia was no longer a more-refined, but merely a more-powerful version of the 'nation-state' concept – led into blind alleys, from which there seemed to be but one possible escape: A headlong flight into imperialist adventurism.[80]

Seen from this angle, the subsequent collapse of democratic Prussia under Otto Braun in the summer of 1932 was simply part of Germany's overall decline under a tidal wave of nationalistic sentiment. Now, more so than at any other time, the Prussian state – thrown onto its own resources – was no longer strong enough to curb dangerous developments within the national context by counteracting the decay of political order and averting the threat of imminent chaos. It was to become apparent that, given any increase in conflict, Prussia would be unable to assert its independence against the *Reich*. Ultimately, whatever fate was to befall Germany, it was to befall Prussia, too.

The outcome was a depressing confirmation of the prophecy – intended in a completely different way at the time it was made – by Fontane that, if seriously propositioned, Prussia would have to be drawn into Germany.[81] The Hohenzollern state put up no resistance against the *Reich* as Chancellor von Papen dealt his blow to Otto Braun's Prussian government and did away with the 'republican stronghold' on 20 July 1932.[82] To charge democratic Prussia with not having had sufficient desire to assert itself, is to fail to recognise that all the domestic prerequisites for mounting effective resistance against the *Reich* had long since disappeared. Although Otto Braun's policy for Prussia was original, matters had already gone too far for any kind of firm stance to be adopted. The combination of a Social Democratic government in Prussia, with a German-National or National Socialist government in the *Reich*, was simply not possible.[83]

In this respect, when a year later, in the course of Hitler's 'standardisation' (*Gleichschaltung*) of *Reich* and *Länder*, Prussia was finally crushed, this was merely an epilogue to the whole drama of Prussian–German history.[84] Inwardly, Prussia had long been 'standardised' and had run out of independent political alternatives to the development of the *Reich*. Moreover, even the forces opposed to a National Socialist *Grossdeutsche Reich* were no longer rallying under the banner of the Prussian cause. Although sections of the Resistance did commemorate the Old-Prussian virtues of sobriety and simplicity, none of them fought against Hitler with the aim of re-establishing Prussia.[85] The Officers' Plot of 20 July 1944 was not a Prussian moment in history, despite the significant role played in it by remarkable men with Prussian names.

This represents a further justification of the formal dissolution of the Prussian state with which postwar Germany's political reconstruction commenced.[86] It was now possible to build a balanced federalistic structure of *Länder*, in the western part of Germany at least, thereby avoiding the evil of having any one state become topheavy. It is, however, important to emphasise that the defeat of Hitler's Germany brought to an end not just Prussia, but also the *Reich*. Both shared the same fate. What was left was not simply a Germany diminished by the loss of Prussia – the Confederation of the Rhine, the clerical republic of which Rathenau had been afraid – but a juxtaposition of two German states. Both contain Prussian elements – different ones, admittedly – and both have to examine certain issues arising from Prussian–German history, issues from which which no-one can escape.

6 ❖ *PRUSSIA: how European was it?*

To assert that Prussia had a perpetually strained relationship with Germany is not to say that it was therefore particularly favourably inclined towards Europe. Conflicts with Germany alone were not enough to predispose Prussia towards Europe. This was all the more true since the concepts of Germany and Europe were never simply geographical ciphers; they always embodied a variety of possible intellectual and political attitudes, as well.[1]

In this respect, it was essential to establish how loosely the concept of Europe might be interpreted. Was it to be equated with notions of 'the West', or did it extend beyond that? There is no unequivocal answer available. The French, for example, tend to refer more to Europe than to the West when seeking, as at present, to defend themselves from an eastern threat. The Anglo-Saxons, on the other hand, prefer to use the concept of the West when describing their political and cultural position. The French usage, *il faut faire l'Europe*, so often heard in current political debate, is virtually impossible to translate into English.[2]

During the nineteenth century, the line of conceptual distinction ran somewhat differently. On the one hand, there were what were known as the 'Western Powers' (*les puissances occidentales*), nations favouring liberalism and opposed to the conservative monarchies of the Holy Alliance. On the other hand, there was the less precise, multi-faceted concept of 'Europe', which could mean variously a cultural idea, a constellation of political power or a geographical area, according to one's requirements. Its

73

elusive quality was described almost cynically by Bismarck in the Varzin *Diktat* of November 1876:

I have always found the word 'Europe' being spoken by those politicians who demand of other nations that they do what they themselves have never dared to do – for example, the western powers during the Crimean War and during the Polish Crisis of 1863, or Thiers in the autumn of 1870 and Count Beust, when summing up the failure of his attempts at coalition against us: *Je ne vois plus l'Europe*.[3]

It is not only Europe which poses problems of definition; the same is true of Prussia, which is not easily demarcated and whose identity was probably clear only unto itself. Although, before the *Reich* was founded, there was no actual danger of Prussia's being amalgamated into Germany, the German world was already reaching into Prussia: through its culture, its social order, its ideals of justice, not least through the *Deutscher Bund* and, earlier, the old German Empire – which were indeed unavoidable realities. Even the most committed Prussian opponent of the *Reich* could not escape the fact that his land was not free of all ties with Germany; no matter who was laying claim to the royal crown in faraway Königsberg, Prussia had no history independently of Germany's history.[4]

Prussia's relations with Europe were therefore never free from German undertones, never completely free from the tensions governing Germany's special path, the German *Sonderweg*. And yet the subject of 'Prussia and Europe' opens up perspectives which a man such as Troeltsch, fearful that Germany would become estranged from the rest of the world, basically failed to notice.[5] Prussia had more in common with the old European world and thus had greater access to the West than was ever suggested by twentieth-century conceptual tussles over 'German culture' and 'western civilisation'. Furthermore, there were phases of history when 'Europe' was for Prussia a counterweight against Germany, a forcefield allowing the ambitious state stretching from the Lower Rhine to the Memel to acquire its own contours both *vis-à-vis* and within the diffuse *monde germanique*, a world as sinister to the French as the 'dreadful German language' was to Mark Twain.[6]

How, then, did 'Europe' encounter Prussia; at what point was it noticed? In seeking to answer this question, it is worthwhile starting with the most straightforward – or, at any rate, most obvious – factor determining a state's historical location: its geographical basis, usually a good guide to its political orientation.[7] This is particularly valid for Prussia which, from the early seventeenth century onwards, had ceased to be an ordinary territorial state of the Holy Roman Empire of the German nation. Having acquired the Prussian Duchy east of the Vistula, it now spread into an area subject to Polish rule. Though the Great Elector managed to liberate this area from Polish feudal authority in 1660, it remained outside the boundaries of the old Empire, and would have to prove itself against the rest of the European powers.[8]

This expansionary move was spectacularly reinforced by the Great Elector's successor, with royal status being bestowed upon the capital of this distant Prussian Duchy at the Coronation in Königsberg in 1701. The choice of Königsberg meant that the King had won his new royal status not on the battlefields of the *Reich* and not through solely German domestic rivalry with the Empire in Vienna, but instead largely independently, on the battlefield of Europe. Rather like the Elector of Saxony, who a few years earlier had acquired the Polish crown, the Brandenburg Elector established, with the crown in Königsberg, a claim which was not based exclusively on *Reich* sources.[9]

This incursion further into Europe was continued under Frederick the Great. In 1772, with the annexation of West Prussia following the first Polish partition, Prussia acquired an additional area not belonging to the old German *Reich*, thus pointing towards a larger constellation: the world of the European powers. With the addition of East and West Prussia, a good quarter of Hohenzollern territory now lay outside the boundaries of the *Reich*, containing a correspondingly large proportion of its total population. Families such as the Dönhoffs and the Dohnas thought as much about Warsaw and Riga as they did about Vienna or the highly-Lutheranised regions of central and northern Germany.[10] Prussia became even further estranged from the *Reich* when it acquired, during the second and third Polish partitions, the wide landscapes of central Poland as far as Bug and Narew. Even though this was but a brief interlude, lasting until Napoleon's reorganisation of Europe, it still lent weight to Prussia's claim to be not only a German, but also a European power. With the additional Polish areas, Prussia almost became a second Habsburg monarchy, a European multinational state.[11]

Nevertheless, the connection with Poland was so strong that it largely withstood the Napoleonic defeat; the official ruling by the Congress of Vienna allowed Prussia to keep Posen and West Prussia – most important of the partition areas for the alignment of Prussia's borders. With Eastern Prussia, of course, it retained an old key area outside of the *Reich*. What was crucial to its position among the other European powers, however, was the fact that none of these regions belonged to the German Confederation. This gave Prussia – rather like Hungary *vis-à-vis* the Habsburg monarchy – the basis of a claim extending beyond Germany, legitimising its position as a European great power.[12]

Within this framework laid down by the Congress of Vienna, Prussia did find something of an opportunity to distinguish itself in Europe from the rest of Germany's small and medium-sized states, to 'free itself from the Federal Philistines' rope', as Bismarck later put it during the 1850s.[13] Here was a platform for a higher plane of politics, or – to paraphrase Heine's comment on the value of Christian baptism to the Jews – an admission ticket to the great powers' club. From this angle, European politics differed from German politics as top-level ones differed from low-level ones; they guaranteed higher status. During the Schleswig-Holstein controversy, Bismarck made this abundantly clear in a letter sent to Count v.d. Goltz, Prussian envoy to Petersburg:

The question is whether we are a major power or a German Federal state, and, if we are the former, whether we are a monarchy or, as is permissible with the latter, whether we should be governed by professors, county judges and small-town windbags.[14]

To Prussia, then, Europe meant a position of enhanced importance. Matters relating solely to Germany were not enough to slake Prussia's thirst for reputation, and only bogged it down in petty obligations. European politics, however, offered greater freedom of decision making, opening up wider scope for action. With a ticket to Europe in its hand, Prussia could even put pressure on the other German states, if need be.[15]

But this view of Europe does not tell us much about Prussia's relationship with the intellectual and social values regarded as the basis of the old Europe and whose influence critical observers of Germany's 'special path', such as Troeltsch, so anxiously sought within the realm of German culture. Simple membership of the circle of European major powers does not guarantee in itself a common heritage, much less an inner bond with Europe as the basis of a particular historical culture. If that were so, there would be no question as to what extent Russia – indubitably one of Europe's major powers – is to be considered European.[16] Here, too, certain points must be raised, before various opinions are discussed. Tracing European values means first having to examine the institutional and social foundations of emotional structures, first having to uncover the realities of experience before assessing the rarified world of ideas. In other words, what were the old European institutions in Prussia like? How 'European' did Prussian society appear?

It is not irrelevant to the issue to discover that this sort of question was never actually asked before the nineteenth century. It did not occur to observers of the Hohenzollern territories prior to the French Revolution that there was anything problematical about Prussia's relationship with Europe. Voltaire, for example, had no doubts that the state led by Frédéric le Grand was a natural part of the European cultural world, although he both knew and saw that court life differed quite considerably to that spent in the country.[17] Mirabeau, too, in his highly critical work co-written with Mauvillon, *De la Monarchie Prussienne*, refused to accept that Prussia, with all its failings, was nothing more than an aberrant form of general European conditions. The first volume, published in London in 1788, states:

... il est incontestable que l'énorme disproportion de l'armée à la population est un mal, un très grand mal; mais ce n'est pas la méthode du recrutement national que l'on en peut accuser; c'est le système politique de l'Europe, la périlleuse situation des provinces prussiennes, et le peu de contiguïté des parties qui composent cette monarchie.[18]

Mirabeau even managed to excuse Prussia's much-despised militarism by placing it within a European context. 'Le système politique de l'Europe' represented the broad framework which Prussia may perhaps have stretched, but never completely nullified or abandoned; the military state of Prussia remained within the boundaries of Europe's rules, notwithstanding its recruitment practices which Mirabeau found so abhorrent. The thought that this very militarism could put Prussia outside of Europe did not cross his mind.[19]

Tocqueville was even more emphatic about Prussia's European aspect, a view remarkable not least because it anticipated the nineteenth-century perspective. In other words, there were already indications here of an awareness of certain specifically German developments. Thus, Tocqueville – not unacquainted with Hegel – was critical of the idiosyncratic nature of German thought, being particularly hostile towards moral-free objectivity. 'Les Allemands . . .', he wrote, in a letter to Gobineau, 'ont seuls en Europe la particularité de se passionner pour ce qu'ils regardent comme la vérité abstraite, sans s'occuper de ses conséquences pratiques.'[20]

Yet Tocqueville's critique of German thought did not alter his opinion about the European foundations of the states that produced it. On the contrary, the great political and social analyst saw a vast Europe of institutions, stretching from the 'borders of Poland to the Irish Sea' and exhibiting remarkably similar institutions in all major spheres. In chapter four of his first volume on *The Ancien Régime and the Revolution*, he described, with evident sympathy, 'comme presque toute l'Europe avait eu précisément les mêmes institutions, et comment ces institutions tombaient en ruine partout'; corporate institutions, property ownership and social dependencies were principally the same throughout Europe, as he saw it.[21]

Within this very broad European context, Prussia did appear to have one particular idiosyncrasy. Tocqueville called Prussia under Frederick the Great a curious combination of 'tête moderne' and 'corps gothique', a political and social hybrid made up of elements dating from the *ancien régime* within a new, thoroughly up-to-date legal system – the General Legal Code. 'La vieille constitution de l'Europe n'est pas assez ruinée dans cette partie de l'Allemagne pour que Frédéric croie, malgré le mépris qu'elle lui inspire, qu'il soit encore temps d'en faire disparaître les débris.'[22]

For Tocqueville, the part of the *ancien régime* retained by Prussia under the General Legal Code was 'la vieille consti-tution de l'Europe', the world of Estates and social inequalities developed in the Middle Ages and common to all European countries. Whilst it therefore linked Prussia with the other states of Europe, it at the same time marked Prussia off from the rest on account of its modern form. Prussia was thus distinct from France because the 'old European constitution' was not simply abolished and wiped out by revolution; it was distinct from the other states – and from those in Germany, above all – because the *ancien régime* no longer went unchallenged, but was subject to the laws of progress. Prussia was thus, according to Toqueville, becoming an interesting variant of the European constitutional system.[23]

In terms of peoples' actual lives and experiences, however, the Prussian version of European constitutionalism was not as consciously European as historical and political analysis might suggest. The nobility faced conflicts surrounding the subject of reform to the Estates system not as gradual departures from a European norm, but instead as a social challenge. Equally, the insurgent urban middle classes scarcely regarded the continual undermining of the *ancien régime* as a decline in Europe's importance, or as a shift in favour of the developing nation-states, for example. The Estates system was far less crucial to Prussia's membership of Europe, than democracy later became in determining the political orientation of states and nations.[24]

Only after the French Revolution – to a certain extent, in reaction to it – was there any tendency to regard certain political attitudes or values as being, to a varying degree, 'European'. The Romantic Movement, in particular, contrasted the modern nation-state with old corporate Europe and thus attributed a greater volume of European traditions to pre-revolutionary systems.[25] Prussia, however, benefited little from such comparisons. Although it was not a nation-state and thus could have been shown as a European alternative to standard European structures, it profited nothing from the Romantic argument. Not even the Gerlach brothers – waging a struggle against the 'Moloch' of the nation-state – were able to make a convincing job of emphasising that Prussia's special qualities as a pre-nation-state were therefore European qualities. Even they (the Gerlachs) went no further than to describe Prussia as a useful element in the 'concert européen' of the Holy Alliance. If any 'European' alternative to the modern nation-state were to be offered at all, then Austria was by far the best candidate.[26]

Conversely, though, as regards a new humanitarian and generally progressive Europe, Prussia was not regarded as being particularly 'European'. Whilst the reputation of the great Enlightenment monarch, Frederick II, survived into the nineteenth century, it was not enough to set the Hohenzollern state amongst the ranks of pioneering, internationalist and universalist order-systems. Prussia was not considered to be an upholder of the ideas born of 1789. Saint-Simon, for instance, in his controversial *De la réorganisation de la société européenne*, published in 1814, made absolutely no acknowledgement whatsoever of Frederick's state; this was a European society centred exclusively on England and France, later including Germany in its entirety. No mention was made of the peoples of eastern central Europe.[27]

During the nineteenth century, therefore, a strange fate befell Prussia. Neither the Romantics, nor the progressive thinkers saw it as a particularly European alternative to the dominant trend towards nation-states. Neither the Holy Alliance, nor the liberal Western powers conceived of Prussia as a viable counterpart or ideological alternative. And yet the latter was by no means a complete misfit within the European order; on the contrary, it was, as Ranke put it, 'naturally European',[28] retaining a position within the concert of European powers because it was so firmly rooted in their traditions. To Hegel, Prussia's naturally European position was related to its Protestantism; in his view, it was as a Protestant power that 'Frederick the Great ushered Prussia in among the mighty nations of Europe'.[29]

But Protestantism in itself was still not sufficient to lend Prussia a European dimension and thus raise it from the German to the European level. The majority of Germany's small states were also Protestant, and because of their denominational inwardness, they tended to be cut off from Europe as a whole. What did give Prussia a European hallmark was far more its own particular brand of Protestantism, originally from outside Germany: Geneva Calvinism. With their conversion to the Reformed faith early in the seventeenth century, the Hohenzollerns had not only advanced history by strengthening active Protestant resistance to the Catholic Counter-Reformation, they had also set in motion significant political impetus, for, by embracing Calvinism, they were opening the doors to the spirit of Western Europe, leading Prussia out of the provincial cul-de-sac of German Lutheranism.[30] The conversion to Calvinism brought Prussia a step closer to Holland and to the world of the French Huguenots. It created a situation whereby, from the Thirty Years War onwards, a growing number of religious refugees, fleeing the European Counter-Reformation, poured into the sparsely-inhabited areas between the River Spree and Memel. By 1700, every third inhabitant of Berlin was French.[31]

Undoubtedly, the House of Brandenburg's conversion did not sever all of Prussia's links with German Lutheranism; the Estates had remained Lutheran. But as the position of Calvinists grew stronger, this helped to prevent Lutheranism from becoming isolated, self-preoccupied or presumptuous even, as it did in

Saxony or Württemberg. In Prussia, Luther almost invariably came up against competition. This was particularly evident during anniversary celebrations of the Reformation. In Prussia, the German reformer never achieved quite the same monopoly-position that he held in the purely Lutheran areas of Germany. During the seventeenth century, Luther was obliged to share the field with Calvin and was judged according to the progress made by the Reformation. The eighteenth century witnessed the crucial issue of practical demonstration of faith, a matter which forbade any glorification of Luther as a person. Even during the nationalistic nineteenth century, Prussia's Reformation anniversaries were different to other German commemorations in that the founding of the Union, on the 300th anniversary of Luther's 95 Propositions, served as a reminder of the Reformation's broader context.[32]

Prussia's modification of Luther should not simply be regarded as an innate and unchanging sign of receptiveness towards supra-German, European ideas. At most, the seventeenth century – with its departure from Lutheranism – may be regarded as an attempt to escape the narrow provincialism of Germany's small-state system. This can be proven to be true of the Great Elector.[33] Apart from this example, its effects were only indirect, stemming from the catalyst of sectarian policies, distinguishing Prussia from the other German states. Given the extent to which Prussia was preparing itself to outgrow the world of German mini-states, it must have been imperative to bolster its dynamism by winning over various forces at the hub of sectarian developments. These did not have to be just the West European Calvinists, they could equally well be Pietists critical of Lutheranism. Thus, in adopting a profile which was no longer exclusively Lutheran-German, Prussia was becoming far more accessible to non-German Europeans.[34]

Nevertheless, Hegel was not completely wrong when he made the figure of Frederick the Great, above all others, give Prussia a European dimension, using a broadly-based definition of Protestantism. Only after the Enlightenment had been incorporated into Prussian state interests was a link with the modern European world finally established; only after sectarian thinking had been fundamentally revised and the principle of tolerance firmly anchored in law did the rest of Europe start to divert its intellectual and spiritual attention towards Prussia. According to Hegel, because Frederick 'had a secular conception of Protestant principles', he reached a 'public' that was to spread Prussia's significance far beyond its actual state boundaries.[35] Public interest also grew partly on account of Prussia's greater scope for manoeuvre in the field of power politics. Prussia also won its place in Europe because it 'withstood' both the might of rival German states and 'the might of almost all of Europe'.[36] In its struggle for existence, Prussia proved itself to be a 'natural part of Europe', to quote Ranke's Hegelian expression once again.

Yet this 'natural part of Europe' was not to shine for long. As Europe battled with the French Revolution, Prussia first faltered, then stood aside and finally, having isolated itself, was completely overcome. The defeats at Jena and Auerstedt were in many ways the penalty Prussia paid for its indecision. It had not wished to ally itself with Napoleonic France, nor had it been prepared to join the European coalition against the latter. During Europe's fateful hours, Prussia was neither progressively European nor conservatively European, but believed that it could remain neutral.[37]

Was it true then, that – in European terms – Prussia was neither fish nor fowl, as numerous critics have repeatedly suggested? Did its neutral position during the crucial years of change express a deep-seated wish to run away from the issues facing Europe? This might well be the impression given in Fontane's first major novel *Vor dem Sturm* (Before the Storm). In this story, the hero's father felt obliged to leave Prussia after the signing of the Peace of Basle in 1795. 'Filled with loathing for the Parisian men of terror, he saw the "pact with the regicides" as just as much a threat to Prussia as a defeat.'[38] Bismarck also saw fit to criticise Prussia's policy of neutrality, in chapter twelve of his *Reflections and Reminiscences*, although his primary concerns were not the same as those expressed by the representative of the

squirearchy in Fontane's noel.[39] Clearly, even by the latter part
of the nineteenth century, Prussia's deviation during Europe's
hour of need was still felt to be an embarrassment.

Before long, however, the nineteenth century blunted the
edge of this particular crisis. Following Napoleon's defeat,
reconciliation rather than opposition was the order of the day.
For the time being, Prussia was able to bask relatively safely in
the 'carp pond of Europe', as Bismarck later acidly called it,[40]
secure in its own identity and untroubled by any question of
what to do, if new conflicts were to erupt. Anyone reading, for
example, the reports submitted by Chateaubriand during his
brief spell as envoy to Berlin during the 1820s, would form the
impression that Prussia had resolved to bring itself down to the
lowest common denominator of European values and order.[41]

European solidarity only became a problem once again when
the anti-Napoleonic front faded, being replaced by others, most
notably one that was located between the Western powers
increasingly receptive towards liberal ideas, and the staunchly
conservative Eastern powers of the Holy Alliance. Under this
new constellation – from 1830 onwards, an increasingly effective
one – Prussia was obliged, more than the other major powers, to
take a good look at its basic policy *vis-à-vis* its allies, and at the
inter-relations between its domestic and its foreign policy. Both
Britain and France, on the one hand, as well as Russia and
Austria, on the other, were far better placed than Prussia was to
arrive at certain clear options, even though their social structures may have been more obviously based on staunchly liberal
or conservative positions. For them, the concept of Europe
nearly always carried associations that tied in with their own
political interests.[42]

Thanks to its geographical location and its social structure,
Prussia was – in contrast – dealing with such heterogeneous
forcefields that it was only able to pursue the concrete notion of a
European order by jeopardising its own vital interests. With a
thoroughly progressive Rhineland province closer to liberal
France than to its own conservative eastern region, and with
'East Elbia' closely linked – not least through the partition of

Poland – with agrarian Eastern Europe, Prussia was torn between a Europe of human rights and a Europe of the old order. Both were Europe, after all, and both stood for traditions which justly claimed to be European. It was not a matter of deciding between Europe and the Orient, it was – to paraphrase Tocqueville – a question of *l'Ancien Régime ou la Démocratie*.

In this situation, Prussia – and not just Bismarck – shied away from making any political mileage out of the concept of Europe. In so doing, perhaps vacuums were allowed to develop, later to be filled by genuinely anti-European forces. Maybe certain German tendencies to deal in politics whilst ignoring general values and rules were bolstered. At bottom, though, Prussia's overall caution about Europe and European links was certainly not part of any kind of deliberate plan to break away from the European system.

Signs of tension between 'Prussia and Europe' – in the sense of a 'Germany versus the West' opposition, resolved by the First World War – did not appear, if at all, until after the founding of the *Reich*. Only when linked, by the new *Reich*, to the Germans, did Prussia begin to develop a more common identity and ideology, sharing the latters' preferences and aversions. Yet an important distinction between them remained: whilst the relationship between Germany and the West rapidly acquired the dimensions of an ideologically-heightened conflict of values, Prussia's relations with Europe remained embedded in old patterns of power rivalry. They still had an old-fashioned, almost outmoded air about them, all the more so since the new *Reich* was beginning to unfold new ambitions for *Weltpolitik*. Prussia's European aspect was ultimately nothing more than the continuation of its pre-Wilhelmine traditions, which admittedly contained the seeds of potential resistance in times of imperialist adventures. To the resistance fighters of 20 July 1944, the memory of Prussia's old-European connections was still enormously relevant.

7 ✤ *PRUSSIA: what was its church like?*

Prussia's church history fares little better than its social history: both tend to be overshadowed by its political history.[1] No matter which century is under consideration, it is always analysed largely in terms of the state and the latter's power apparatus. Church history appears extraordinarily dull by comparison. A handful of isolated phenomena are, perhaps, reasonably well-known, such as August Hermann Francke's group of Halle Pietists, or else the Awakening Movement in Pomerania and Silesia during the Romantic period. Little is known about the church as an institution, however; there is no comprehensive study of Prussian ecclesiastical history available.[2]

This omission is particularly glaring with regard to the Protestant Church. Whilst the Catholic Church has always managed to retain an identity independently of the state, emerging from conflicts such as the *Kulturkampf* as a political factor in its own right, the Protestant Church – although for a long time the official church – has always remained within the shadow of the state. This situation brought out real symptoms of weakness when, for instance, during the settlement of the *Kulturkampf* foremost Protestants feared that their church would suffer neglect as a result of the Prussian government's excessive concessions to the Catholic Church.[3] Bismark felt obliged to answer this change, spelling out the exact position: 'Equality of the two churches in the state of Prussia is . . . impossible by their very natures: they are incommensurable qualities . . . Whilst the King of Prussia remains head of the Protestant Church, there can be no question of formal equality between the two churches'.[4]

Bismarck not only outlined the distinction between the positions occupied by both major churches, he also took the opportunity of reminding Protestant spokesmen of the fundamental hierarchical order that governed Prussia's church/state relations: 'Originally, the Protestant Church enjoyed hospitality as a guest in the house of the state of Prussia. In time, it has acquired joint-ownership of the house, but the original owner was always the Prussian state.'[5]

There was no doubt, therefore, about the order of rank in Prussia: The state came first, followed then by the church. This had a number of repercussions, not least for the Protestant Church, which had certain obligations to the state.[6] Not only did it owe its legal structure to the territorial ruler – who had presided, from the outset, as its highest bishop, *'summus episcopus'* – it also relied heavily upon the state for financial support. As the established church of the *Land* and, later, of the state, it derived countless benefits from a close association with Prussia's temporal rulers. There was, however, a high price to be paid: an ever-greater loss of autonomy. In his 'Introduction' to the commemorative work published by the Supreme Church Council of the Old-Prussian Union, Otto Dibelius – Prussian conservative Bishop of Berlin – summed up how 'whenever the interests of the state threatened to clash with those of the church, the state naturally held priority'. Not until the nineteenth century was it at last 'realised that a country's "church" cannot be administered in the same way as the royal forests or the state archives'.[7] But how had this situation come about?

The earliest influence on the structure of Prussia's Protestant Church was the degree of ecclesiastical jurisdiction acquired by secular territorial rulers at the time of the Reformation.[8] In Prussia, as in the majority of German territories affected by the Reformation, a shortage of reformist bishops meant that the role of 'stand-in bishop' fell to the territorial ruler, an arrangement which led to the establishment of the latter's position as highest bishop. Whilst the Brandenburg Electors of the sixteenth century were subject to considerable restrictions upon their secular rule because of the Estates, they enjoyed a marked increase in influence and authority within church affairs.[9] A Consistory, appointed in 1543, granted them administrative powers over the Lutheran Church, which had no governing committees of its own other than several experimental attempts at establishing pastoral synods at the local level, and the temporary office of General superintendent.

Most important of all, perhaps – although the full extent of its repercussions was not apparent at the time – was the fall in numbers on the clerical benches of the *Landtag*.[10] With the secularisation of the monasteries and the loss of dioceses, the basis for a separate *curia* of prelates had crumbled. There were no longer enough representatives from the cathedral chapters, abbeys and bishoprics to constitute an independent clerical Estate. A few members of secularised cathedral chapters for a time retained an association with the Knights' Estate, but this did not alter the fact that, thereafter, the clergy was no longer represented in the *Landtag* alongside the nobility and the burghers' Estates.[11]

This – apparently natural – side-effect of the Reformation was to have far-reaching consequences. They not only touched upon the very socio-economic foundations of the church, they also had a lasting effect upon its self-image. Until then, the church had been highly conscious of being a separate Estate within the world of princes, knights and burghers. From then on, however, it was to regard itself increasingly as just part of the territorial princes' apparatus for rulership, an adjunct or, at best, a complement to their rule. Thereafter, deprived of its own political representation, the church would lose both a great deal of autonomy and an increasing amount of self-confidence socially, to the point where it could no longer recognise the contours of its own social and political identity within the outside world.[12]

Not even a growing consciousness of official dignity on the part of the new Protestant clergy could compensate for this. Although the pastor's house rapidly became a focal point for the general improvement of manners and education, the pastor's actual dependence upon the individual patron still prevented him from developing any real sense of social muscle. The office was not in itself an automatic passport to status, particularly since the Protestant clergy came, as a rule, from bourgeois families lacking in social standing,[13] and hardly ever from the nobility. With the offices of abbot and bishop having been abolished, the nobility evidently felt that the church could no longer offer any socially acceptable career openings at all. At any rate, they held themselves aloof from the Protestant clergy and made no attempts to share any plans they may have had.

This situation lasted not simply for the first hundred years of the Protestant Church's existence; it grew still worse in the aftermath of the Thirty Years War, and led to unmistakable signs of social regression amongst the clergy.[14] Even at the height of the Pietist era, when sections of the nobility resumed a greater interest in questions of faith, if not in forms of Lutheran piety, prominent members of Prussia's ecclesiastical circles, such as the Berlin Court preacher, Daniel Ernst Jablonski, publicly deplored the lack of social prestige associated with his calling:

It is well known that in Prussia no-one of even moderately high social standing can allow their sons to study theology . . . although some preachers may do everything possible to encourage boys with an interest in the subject to take up these studies, by the time they are old enough to appreciate the current predicament of the clergy, they change their minds, opting for secular positions and occupations instead. As a result, those who do devote themselves to the service of the Lord are, of necessity, people from the lower classes, lacking in both an education and the means to acquire one. In order to subsist, they are obliged to work as private tutors to other families. Having mastered neither scholarly learning nor the rules of orderly conduct, they cannot fail to be a disgrace – rather than a credit – to their holy office. Small wonder that public morals are on the decline and that sin and profanity go unchecked. With theologians such as these to represent it, the vocation cannot but be despised.[15]

The critical comments voiced by the Prussian court preacher echo a concern that, without any new blood of adequate social standing, the church would compare badly with the secular world of the state and the Estates. If too large a discrepancy in social prestige were to arise between the servants of the church and those of the state, the church would no longer be in any position to maintain serious and critical dialogue with the latter, or to execute its duties properly. An exclusively middle-class church within a society dominated by the nobility would, according to Jablonski, be in a very awkward situation indeed.

This extra prestige enjoyed by the representatives of the secular powers was an advantage found in other Protestant territories, too. It also strengthened still further the superior position held by the state following the Reformation.[16] It acquired an added dimension in Prussia, however, when, in the seventeenth century, there took place two changes significant to both ecclesiastical and general history. These were the conversion of the Hohenzollern rulers to Calvinism, and the gradual extension of their power beyond the Mark Brandenburg, to create a multi-territorial major State.[17] Both processes were to bring about a fundamental adjustment to the balance of power between church and state, producing a marked shift in favour of the church. The Hohenzollerns' conversion to Calvinism quite considerably widened the distance that lay between Prussia's secular leaders and the circles still loyal to the Lutheran Church, and the latter became increasingly subject to political repression. Moreover, since Calvinism was at that time considered to be the more politically progressive faith, the Lutheran Church gradually acquired an image of being provincial and backward, incapable of keeping pace with the new demands being made by the developing state authority.[18]

This grew all the more apparent once Prussia – by acquiring territory on the Lower Rhine, in East Prussia and, after the Peace of Westphalia, in eastern Pomerania, Halberstadt and Minden, later also Magdeburg – started to outgrow the confines of a simple territorial state. Whilst the state was developing greater calibre, its individual churches seemed provincial in more than just the geographical sense of the word. Politically, too, they were being left behind by the state, which was expanding into new areas of activity, such as consolidating and modernising its scattered territories from the Lower Rhine to the

Memel. In a variety of ways, distinctions between the two
establishments grew: on the one hand, a large-scale, forward-
looking state; on the other, a church system trapped within the
confines of obsolescent Estate structures and of narrow
provincialism.[19]

The question therefore arises as to what, if any, attempts were
made to overcome the discrepancies between church and state
development. Was the church ultimately to fall behind the ever-
stronger modern state, or was it still to find ways of avoiding
slipping even further behind? It is one of the peculiarities of
seventeenth and eighteenth-century Brandenburg–Prussian
history that certain corrective forces – a legacy of the Reformation – were able to act as an antidote to the symptoms of
repression within ecclesiastical life. To begin with, it was in fact
Calvinism – so welcome to the dynasty – which helped to
prevent the church from being regarded as a mere appendage to
the Estates system. Acutely aware of its widespread solidarity,
politically dynamic and with its practice of presbyterial leadership, Calvinism broadened the church's horizons and spawned
progressive competition. It also pierced – in part, at least – the
shell of a largely pugnacious church of theologians which, in the
arena of international debate and conflict, was noted more for
its verbal battles than for its actual presence.[20]

Indirectly, too, Calvinism helped the church in
Brandenburg-Prussia to break out of its limited, Estates-
oriented provincialism. By claiming equal rights with Lutheranism, it took the edge off the prevailing denominationalism,
forcing the Protestant faiths to work towards a policy agreement. It would undoubtedly be wrong to attribute this particular effect of Calvinist policy to deliberate intent; nonetheless,
there can be little doubt that the dynasty's conversion to the
Reformed faith did lead directly to the establishment of religious
tolerance in Brandenburg-Prussia.[21]

It was a process equally important to both ecclesiastical and
secular history, all the more so when Brandenburg-Prussia
absorbed large groups of Reformed Protestants. Initially, with
the acquisition of regions on the Lower Rhine shortly before

the outbreak of the Thirty Years War, Calvinist territories became part of an otherwise Lutheran state. They helped to break
down the traditional association between the corporative state
(*Ständestaat*) and the denominational church, and argued
that the future united monarchic state should pursue a
denominationally-neutral policy for its churches. Secondly,
with the tremendous influx of refugees of the Reformed faith
after the Thirty Years War and, above all, of French Huguenots
following the Edict of Potsdam in 1685, an ecclesiastical policy
without the principle of religious tolerance became an
impossibility.[22]

Yet Calvinism was not to be the sole corrective force against
the retarded nature of the Lutherans' denominationalist
church; Lutheranism itself spawned certain impulses from
within, bringing to ecclesiastical life an altogether greater
importance in the eyes of state and of society: This was the
revivalist movement known as Pietism.[23] From its inception
highly critical of the Estates, the movement grew up in Halle, at
the new university, where August Herrmann Francke was
formulating his treatise on practical Christianity. He questioned
the conception which lay behind the prevailing denominationalism of the churches, and was critical of its effects. His notions of
actively proving individual faith contained many seeds of
economic and social reform, which – correctly applied – had
great political potential.[24]

It is a remarkable feature of Brandenburg-Prussian history
that here, it proved possible to harness Pietism – in spite of some
of its fantastical elements – to the cause of the state. Whilst in
other Protestant areas of Germany, the troublesome revivalist
movement was shunted into an ecclesiastical and political
siding, in Prussia it was successfully wooed by the Hohenzollern
rulers, who were planning to incorporate it into the structure of
the state.[25] Thus, Pietism ended up in the same role as that once
played by Berlin Calvinism, counteracting the Estates-oriented
denominationalism which was no longer useful to the developing monarchical, unified state.

Far from countervailing the growing power of Absolutism,

however, the Brandenburg-Prussian Pietists were increasingly drawn, just like the members of the Reformed faith, into the ambit of the state's power-aspirations, so much so that they ultimately came into conflict with their original principles. Without actually arguing, as Marxist critics have done, that Pietism served as an internal pillar of Prussian Absolutism,[26] it should still be recognised that this important revivalist movement was critical only of the Estates, not of the state; it capitulated before the institutions of the military, Absolutist state.

If one questions the contribution made by the two 'modern' offshoots of Protestant Christianity, Calvinism and Pietism, in creating the modern state, one reaches an ambivalent conclusion. On the one hand, it has to be admitted that, in their different ways, both tendencies did help to overcome or, at least, reduce resistance to the construction of the modern state in its Prussian form. Indirectly, too, they also helped to pave the way for tolerance with regard to church policy, thereby setting a precedent for greater freedom generally. On the other hand, though, there can be no denying that neither Calvinism nor Pietism were able to counteract the repressive aspects of the Prussian military state or to generate any kind of preliminary criticism of Absolutism. Unlike their Western European counterparts, they failed to spark off any impulses for dissent.[27]

There were several explanations for this. One of the most important was the complete lack of organisational autonomy granted to Calvinism and Pietism, making it difficult for them to maintain any distance from the state. Even the self-confident Calvinist movement, well-aware of the importance of institutions, was unable to get any independent synodal structures set up in the regions governed by the squirearchy east of the River Elbe, or to discover any feasible alternatives to the patriarchal world of Lutheranism.[28] On the contrary, Calvinism in many ways made the churches even more dependent upon the state; tied, by faith, to the ruling dynasty, it bent itself entirely to the latter's will, and considered reform from above to be the most promising means for the church to achieve success.

Although, with the Hohenzollerns' conversion to Calvinism, a certain distance had grown between Prussia's rulers and its established church , the former did not in any way loosen their hold over the latter. Indeed, it was the secession of the faiths which caused the sovereign's authority over the church to be substantially diminished, which in turn helped to further the formal development of a state church.[29]

This process was considerably accelerated by the Calvinists and – with certain reservations – subsequently by the Pietists, too. In attempting to eradicate denominational particularism, their success matched that of the state in its battle against Estate particularism, even though, in individual regions, Lutheran consistories did continue to exist. Initially, it was simply a matter of establishing central ecclesiastical authorities for the whole state, but this soon necessitated a co-ordination of the clerical and civil administrations, in the process of which the church – as an autonomous entity – fell by the wayside. In the end, the highest ecclesiastical office was allocated to a Department of Clerical Affairs allied to the judiciary.[30]

The attitude adopted by Prussia's Protestant Church during the Age of Enlightenment must be viewed against this particular background. It was an attitude which – despite all the basic influence of theology[31] – was profoundly affected by the prevailing circumstances regarding the constitution of the churches. These at least made it easier for the churches to be receptive towards the spirit of the Enlightenment. As the concept of the church gradually became empty of denominational and theological content, there was every opportunity for an adjustment of the church as such, for fundamental criticism which was part of the Enlightenment's belief in Rationalism. Since the church was still only permitted to be seen as just another organ of the state, it was inevitably regarded as a useful channel for promoting decent behaviour and welfare, a kind of social agency!

In this respect, it was precisely in Prussia that the standards and values of the established state church, and those held by the nascent bourgeois society grew very similar to each other. The boundaries dividing church duties from those of the state were largely blurred, so that a leading churchman of the Frederician period, the Reformed court Preacher August Friedrich Wilhelm Sack, could be confident of gaining general approbation when he remarked: 'Oh, how absolute and complete the happiness of a people would be, amongst whom true Christianity, leading to the practice of all social virtues, were also supported, not given orders or hindered, by civil law!'[32]

What, though, if civil law were governed by another spirit altogether, with aims different to those held by church leaders? Such was the case during the controversy surrounding the Woellner Edict on Religion, promulgated two years after the death of Frederick the Great.[33] With this edict – a deliberate reaction to the so-called free thinking of the Frederician era – Woellner, a Rosicrucian sympathiser and Minister of the Clerical Department, intended to halt Enlightenment incursion into the church. Furthermore, with the help of appropriate administrative measures, he planned 'to protect the Christian faith . . . from all falsification',[34] with action being taken against the 'modish teachings'.

At the formal level, this was perfectly proper, being well within the scope of the territorial ruler's jurisdiction over the welfare of Protestant Church, both '*circa sacra*' and '*in sacra*'.[35] Because, however, the territorial ruler's control over the church had, in the course of time, assumed a more external character, becoming akin to a 'church authority', there was considerable surprise when the ruler's relationship with his churches suddenly reverted to one that was governed by matters of actual content. Most of all, there was widespread consternation when it unexpectedly became apparent that the supposed congruence between church and state was anything but self-evident. It signified, at any rate, that problems could ensue whenever conflicts arose in key areas of both organisations.

In this particular instance, conflict erupted because five members of the Lutheran Upper Consistory,[36] after deliberations as to the advantages and disadvantages brought to the church by the Enlightenment, reached conclusions that differed from those held by the Minister responsible.[37] Expressing reservations against his actions, they voiced their displeasure at the extent to which the state was intervening in affairs which, in their opinion, were the concern of the church and as such, ought certainly to be settled without any outside interference. At the same time, they were growing increasingly aware of a deficit in church autonomy, making opposition to the state exceedingly difficult.[38] In pre-Absolutist times, church policy had still been a fairly clear-cut and separate affair, although it was still supported by the state. Later, state policy had come to be equated automatically with the church, and no clear distinction was made between them. The church thus became nothing more than an executive organ.

This lack of autonomy was a key problem for the Protestant Church, and in Prussia particularly so. In the very birthplace of the Absolutist state, the problem of the risks associated with a state church was also at its most acute. The question arose as to how far, if at all, the church was managing to free itself from the fetters of Absolutism without relapsing into the pre-Absolutist weaknesses of denominationalism and provincialism. Would ecclesiastical affairs, like social and political affairs, undergo a process of emancipation from authoritarian attitudes, or would essential distinctions remain?

This was the issue current after the Stein-Hardenberg reforms of ecclesiastical matters.[39] The Prussian Legal Code had strengthened the principle of state ordinance over the churches, making all 'church societies' subject to state authority.[40] Social change, accelerated by the French Revolution, now made it necessary for the churches' actual position within the state and within society to be scrutinised and more clearly defined, where necessary. The question was whether the churches themselves ought to develop new structures to satisfy changing social and political conditions, and to secure greater autonomy *vis-à-vis* the state.

Within the Protestant Church, the foremost proponent of church reform was Schleiermacher.[41] After his help had been enlisted by Stein, he produced, in 1808, an 'Outline of a New

Ecclesiastical System for the Prussian Monarchy'. This represented a radical break with the notion of the church as a state institution, suggesting several ways in which the Protestant Church might be restructured.[42] It envisaged the church bearing sole responsibility for its own internal affairs, proposed that presbyteries be elected in the parishes, and that synods consisting of clerics be appointed at district (*Kreis*) level. Provincial churches were to be headed by self-administering chapters, presided over by a bishop. Denominational division within the Protestant Church was to become a thing of the past.

Schleiermacher's plan undoubtedly conformed with a great deal of the general political ideals current during the Reform period, notions of wider citizen participation within community and public affairs. Nonetheless, it was rooted in a genuine theological concern about the nature of the church, thinking which also assessed the previous history of Prussia's churches:

There can be no denying that our Church system is in an acute state of decline; active participation in public worship and in holy observances has fallen off almost completely; the influence of religious attitudes upon moral behaviour and the judgement thereof is scarcely detectable; vital relations between preachers and their congregations have virtually dissipated, and so, too, has ecclesiastical discipline. As far as dignity is concerned, the entire clerical Estate is sinking inexorably, and as regards its true vocation, it is caught in a dangerous bout of lethargy. All this trouble stems from some of the mistakes made here in Prussia after the Reformation. Until then, the Church had gone too far in liberating itself from the State and in setting itself above it, even. Thereafter, it has been made excessively subordinate to the State, and it has increasingly come to be thought of as a mere instrument of the State. As a result, there has been far too much judgement of Church affairs by reference to principles of external law and external liability, and inevitably, this has caused its true spirit to be overlooked.[43]

Schleiermacher's ideas were by no means unanimously well-received, though. Stein himself seemed to be sympathetic, but only a few weeks later he was sacked and was therefore unable to help with their implementation.[44]

What did take shape was initially only the section of church reform that related directly to the reform of the highest state authorities, and that was not a great deal. Decrees promulgated in December 1808 merely dissolved Prussia's old clerical institutions, placing all jurisdiction – both supervisory and executive – in the hands of an entirely secular office of the state, the section for Cultural Affairs and Public Education at the Ministry of the Interior.[45] Reform in the ecclesiastical field was even more of a non-starter than it had been in other fields, failing to get beyond a clarification of formal responsibility demarcation. For the time being, it was simply carrying the idea of a state church to extremes.[46]

Although various reforms did eventually get under way, this was undoubtedly because general social and political developments made any further stasis impossible. For one thing, the greatly increased strength of the Catholic Church thanks to Prussia's land gains during and after the Frederician period meant that church/state relations in Prussia were no longer an almost exclusively Protestant affair. Since the Catholic Church was now involved, too, it began to demand more consideration for its specific interests,[47] and thus helped to alter the way in which the territorial ruler governed the Protestant Church. Furthermore, the process of secularisation triggered off by the *Reichsdeputationshauptschluss* of 1803 and furthered, in 1810, by the Prussian Edict on the surrender of church-owned lands forced a reorganisation of ecclesiastical assets.[48] Suffering material losses, the churches were obliged to seek a new basis for autonomy and certainly to pay greater heed to the question of the boundary dividing the concerns of the state from those of the church.

Ultimately, in order that serious institutional discrepancies might be avoided, Hardenberg's civil administrative reforms were finally matched by corresponding church reforms. Thus, as the Prussian state underwent reorganisation in the course of the territorial reshaping of Central Europe instigated by the Congress of Vienna, there seemed to be no other option but to extend the bureaucracy's institutions at the provincial level. This decision, in turn, was to have repercussions upon the church system. The establishment of Senior Committees (*Oberpräsidien*) – complementary to the governments at regional (*Bezirk*) level – in the provinces led to the setting-up of

Provincial Consistories of the church, with responsibility for both cultural affairs and public education.[49] This new kind of consistory was admittedly a far cry from the old-style ones abolished by Stein; they were wholly state authorities under the chairmanship of a Senior President (*Oberpräsident*), with no trace of any independence for the church in running its affairs. Nevertheless, they did form part of a more balanced regional structure which was to become important to the churches' sense of collective identity, and for that of the Protestants particularly.

The crucial question still facing the reformers was whether an administrative reorganisation of the churches would then be followed by any renewal of their internal structure. In the Protestant domain, this was a question of setting up presbyteries and synods.[50] If, at that time, the political arena was dominated by discussion of matters such as local self-administration, a great deal of church debate was also taken up with evaluating the disadvantages and advantages of synodal governing structures. It remained to be seen where these new forms of participation were to encounter the most resistance: in political society, or in ecclesiastical society.

In the Protestant field, this discussion met not only with some very reactionary responses but also with some very different notions of reform. Apart from the people such as Schleiermacher who called for a genuinely synodal structure for the church, with clearly-defined areas of competence for each new committee, there were also the reformers at the Ministry of Education and Cultural Affairs – most notably Nicolovius[51] – keen to consolidate the church system by promoting the clerical Estate and by raising educational standards within the clergy. These reformers were also in favour of synods, but without any say in matters of ecclesiastical administration and certainly not as self-running entities. To men such as Nicolovius, the idea of a self-administering church was entirely unimaginable; they recognised the church not as an institution enjoying its own rights and laws, but as a mere 'organisation' allowed the dignity of attending to the welfare of a state well-aware of the limits of its power.

Thus, an 'Improvement of the Protestant Ecclesiastical

Constitution in Prussia' came about, an improvement bearing only scant resemblance to Schleiermacher's proposals for an independent and self-responsible church. With a Cabinet Order dated May 27 1816, the King gave permission for 'the Protestant clergy of each *Kreis* to form a District Synod chaired by a Superintendent'.[52] Likewise, 'Provincial Synods' were to be formed, consisting of all the superintendents, headed by a general superintendent, meeting 'once or twice a year, as necessary, to discuss the internal clerical affairs of the entire *Provinz*'.[53] There was to be no voting for the post of chairman.

Besides this, the King ordered that 'in each parish, a presbytery or ecclesiastical college be appointed, comprising the clergyman, the patron (where applicable) and several members of the congregation. Their task will be to look after the welfare and the rights of the church.' In order to make clear the precise extent of social change permissible, it was, however, added that all existing rights of suffrage and of patronage were to remain unchanged.[54] The King reserved the right to make exceptions to this rule, as for example in the case of the western provinces reshaped by French rule.

With this decree, the Protestant Church in Prussia was entitled to form committees that were partly complementary to the State's administration of ecclesiastical affairs. In actual character, though, they were vastly different to what the church reformers associated with Schleiermacher had envisaged.[55] Synods had by now become little more than simple conferences of vicars, whilst presbyteries – if convened at all – were a sort of club for the patron and his local clergyman. Like its political counterpart, the Estates General, a General Synod for the entire state of Prussia had still to be created.

Overall, the reorganisation suffered from one particular weakness which was to have a long-term effect upon basic relations between the Church and modern society in Prussia: the absence of any independent lay-element within the structure of the church. At the time of the old corporative state, the local patron was an appropriate form of lay presence within the church. Similarly, during the Absolutist period, the church had acquired non-clerical colleagues in the shape of representatives from the state bureaucracy. During the early constitutional period, however, the church had no secular partners appropriate to the current stage of social development. The Prussian church's dealings with 'the secular world' were via the state and an Estates-oriented society. There were no lay-persons – as free members of bourgeois society – serving on any church committees. The consequence of this was a two-fold weakness: Without any representatives from modern society, the church grew inwardly more clerical than was actually appropriate to Protestant thinking at that time, and became outwardly more dependent upon the state than the impulses of the reform era would have led one to expect. There was thus little potential within the Protestant Church in Prussia for cosmopolitan ecclesiastical self-confidence to develop.

These weaknesses were not removed by any practical policies during the years of restoration, either. Indeed, as in the political sphere, the realisation of institutional reforms was so protracted a process that it was virtually non-existent. It was not until 1818/19 that synods were finally appointed, initially at *Kreis* level and later in the provinces, whilst the establishment of presbyteries proceeded only very haltingly. In both cases, regional distinctions were major considerations. Setting up synods and presbyteries was far easier in the western provinces where traditions had undergone reform, than it was in the Lutheran East Elbian provinces, where such structures were completely unknown. All the same, the west presented difficulties of a different kind, problems for the territorial rule of the church. The newly-established presbyteries and synods began to press for wider powers for the new committees, demanding above all lay-participation in the workings of the synods. They denounced as 'inadequate' the concessions granted by Cabinet Order of 1816.[56]

But in the eastern provinces, too, individual synods were rebelling. Most notably, the provincial synod in Brandenburg – of which Schleiermacher was a member – was campaigning for full synodal rights and was starting to challenge the consistory.[57]

It regarded the Cabinet Order as containing a number of points which had to be developed further. But precisely this brought about the downfall of the synod's initiatives. In a climate dominated by the Karlsbad Decrees, the Prussian government felt the need to clamp down on all constitutional problems and to nip in the bud both the synodal movement and the campaign for universal suffrage. Indeed, the establishment of presbyteries was even revoked.[58]

If, despite these symptoms of regression, the synodal movement did not peter out altogether, this was due not least to a certain episode in church politics, the second major issue in early nineteenth-century Prussian Protestant Church history: the introduction, in 1817 – the anniversary year of the Reformation – of the *Union*.[59] With this, a cause particularly close to the heart of Frederick William III, several interests happened to coincide: first, the state had political reasons for wanting to create a uniform Protestant Church; secondly, numerous leaders of both branches of the Protestant faith, Lutheran and Reformed, were anxious to further the cause of denominational harmony and to bolster the Protestant Church against the growing influence of Catholicism in Prussia; lastly, the Liberals were also keen to help eliminate the denominationalism that was so harmful to the course of progress. This last interest was not actually what the *Union*'s leading proponents themselves wanted, for it seemed to point in the direction of federal co-operatives with political liberalism. Ultimately, though, these impulses all contributed equally towards keeping the topic of Protestant Church reorganisation on the agenda, so that it was not, like so many attempts at political reform, driven from the arena of public debate.

One contributory factor was an ecclesiastical policy dispute arising from the founding of the *Union* in Prussia. This was the controversy surrounding the introduction of a standard liturgy for all the provincial churches in Prussia. The so-called liturgy dispute (*Agendenstreit*)[60] unleashed more passions than the reformers had thought possible, and in the parishes, especially, it made people far more aware of how vital it was for the church to hold responsibility independently of the state. Although much of the resistance to a standard liturgy was prompted by denominationalist provincialism, in rejecting state *dirigisme*, these critics came to share in a common struggle alongside supporters of the synodal movement, who were similarly anxious to impose limits upon the Absolutism of the state church.

This combined struggle – against the liturgy, and for a synodal constitution – found its strongest support in the two western provinces of the Rhineland and Westphalia. Here, the largely Reformed synods, and numerous parishes made their acceptance of changes to the liturgy conditional upon reform of the ecclesiastical constitution, too. In this way, they ultimately got the King to approve an acceptable compromise.[61] With the Rhenish Westphalian Ecclesiastical Decree dated 5 March 1835 – following the earlier acceptance of a revised liturgy – provincial churches were conceded a presbyterial–synodal structure incorporating just one episcopalian element: at the top was not the *Präses* (the elected head of the provincial synod), but instead – as in the other Prussian provinces – the General Superintendent appointed by the King. In all else, the most important principles of synodalism were granted, in so far as both *Kreis* and province synods, as well as the presbyteries, contained elected lay-representatives with voting powers, whilst the synods acquired the right to elect their chairman.[62]

Ecclesiastical disputes persisted, however, in one of the East Elbian provinces, although they concerned a different issue here. In Silesia, numerous congregations loyal to the Lutheran faith grew defensive about the threat of *Union* interference and thus withheld their approval of the standard liturgy[63]. The stimulus which in Rhenish-Westphalian congregations led to a strengthening of their Reformed faith traditions caused the Lutheran Church of Silesia to resist domination by the state, harking back to an independence which began when Silesia was linked to Austria. The resistance in Silesia did not meet with the same success as in the West, however. The King forcibly instituted the revised liturgy, and announced a measure which contrasted strangely with the policies of religious tolerance practised by the Hohenzollerns during the seventeenth and eighteenth centuries: Old-Lutheran rebels were forced to emigrate.[64]

Within the framework of various challenges to the bureaucratic control of the Prussian state church, there was yet another movement of significance, one striving for reform in what was actually a spirit of conservatism: the Pietist Awakening Movement.[65] The Pietists, forming themselves into simple communities transcending both denominational and social barriers, were found within every type of social milieu, from the peasant farm to the aristocracy. They were the basis of groups which – all according to their particular circumstances – challenged the official church from 'below' or from 'above'. In Old-Lutheran circles, they furthered the development of a free church; in Rhenish Reformed circles, they strengthened the parish church element, and at the Royal Court in Berlin, they supported those who wished for the church to be run by its bishops. In every area, the Pietists were opposed to a religiosity that was based on administration, rejecting too close a tie between Church and State.

Church history took a new turn in 1840, with the accession of Frederick William IV.[66] The new King was determined to abandon the old bureaucratic methods by which his father had run both secular and sacred affairs, and wished to introduce more liberal, non-absolutist forms of political life. Much depended, of course, upon the interpretation of 'non-Absolutist'; it was possible to see them as pre-absolutist and Estates-oriented, or, equally, as post-Absolutist and liberal. The basic problem with Frederick William IV's new policy was that it left room for both interpretations and thus aroused hopes in both camps. In terms of ecclesiastical politics, this meant that both the synodal and the episcopal movements felt sufficiently encouraged to mount a new attack on the existing order. In the field of domestic politics, Liberals and Old-Conservatives opposed to the bureaucratic state jointly demanded – albeit from differing motives – that the Estates-dominated *Landtage* be extended, thereby re-opening the constitutional issue.[67] Similarly, the synodalists and episcopalists were oddly united in their call for a greater number of autonomous church institutions at district, province and national level.[68] The demand that a Prussian Estates General – a *Landtag* for the entire state – be convened corresponded to the demand for a General Synod to crown the edifice of a *Landeskirche* for the entire state.

The year 1843 therefore saw the reactivation of clerical *Kreis* synods in the eastern provinces, and 1844 saw the appointment of *Provinz* synods there in an extended form, even. In contrast to 1818, their members included not only superintendents but also one freely-elected clergyman per *Kreis*, together with other representatives from the church and from the theological faculty of the local university. In 1845, the consistorial administration was reorganised, as a result of which, this hitherto temporal authority was handed over to clerical care.[69] In 1846, the renewal process reached a climax when a General Synod for the entire state of Prussia was finally convened. The full significance of this event is best assessed by means of a further comparison with political developments: It was not until a year later that a body of political representatives for the whole state was finally assembled, the United Diet (*Vereinigter Landtag*) of 1847.[70] To a certain extent, therefore, the church showed politicians the way towards establishing a representative committee which, complementary to the existing organs of state, served to develop informed opinion. This accounts for the fact that meetings of the General Synod aroused such great public interest. It also explains the highly emotional tenor of debates which in part fulfilled a distinctly substitute political function.[71]

The General Synod was convened – like the *Kreis* and *Provinzial* synods a few years previously – in the belief that 'the Protestant Church, if it is to be truly and lastingly helped, must be governed not just by the system of ecclesiastical discipline, but primarily must be uplifted by its own inner life and impetus'.[72] The General Synod membership numbered seventy-five – of whom one half were from the laity – appointed by the King either because of their office (General Superintendents,

Consistory Presidents etc.) or else because they had been recommended or elected. Compared with the United Diet, the social composition of the General Synod had a far stronger bias towards university-trained professionals (almost 50% were academic doctors and professors), with not one single representative from the peasantry. Of the twenty-four lay members recommended by the provincial synods, ten were to reach the United Diet within the year: one member of the *Curia* of Peers, seven representatives from the Knighthood, and two Burghers.[73]

In reality, the General Synod was thus an assembly of notables, though this does not alter the fact that the recommendations it made (for it was not permitted to pass any actual resolutions) were astoundingly progressive. On the issue of church constitutional reform, in particular, it made virtually the same demands as those put forward by the synodal movement: gradual introduction of the electoral principle at every level, from the presbyteries to the General Synod; recognition of a limited period in office for all synods; greater responsibilities for the synods, as opposed to the consistories; the establishment of an Upper Consistory as an ecclesiastical counterpart to the secular Ministry of Education and Cultural Affairs.[74] The King, however, saw fit to refuse the synods' demands,[75] as he would also do the following year with the United Diet. In dashing these hopes, he only added to growing political instability as the 1848 Revolution drew nearer.

Thus, for all the numerous efforts that had been made, the year 1848 saw Prussia's Protestant Church still deprived of a constitution that was both independent and in keeping with the times.[76] Unlike middle-class society – which strove increasingly for greater secularisation – Prussis's church was highly uncertain about its own identity and its relationship with the secular world. After a period of tremendous vacillation, it thus ended up being even more dependent upon the ruling powers than ever before. The Revolution did, undoubtedly, create a measure of impetus towards serious consideration of the social question – the most striking example of this being the diverse activities of Johann Hinrich Wichern.[77] As far as any hopes for reforming the church from within were concerned, the revolution unleashed more anxiety than positive encouragement. There were no wholly independent initiatives made towards completing the reform programme presented in 1846, or, even, towards convening a non-governmental 'revolutionary' General Synod, analogous to the Prussian National Assembly. Not even in the provinces was there any campaign for freely-elected synods.[78] The one church assembly to grow from the unrest of 1848 was the so-called Wittenberg Church Congress, concerned less with Prussian than German affairs, such as establishing a German Protestant League of Churches.[79]

To sum up, it must be said that the breakthrough to modern constitutionalism had first to be achieved within political society before the church could proceed with its constitutional development. Without doubt, this was because of the latter's close ties with the structures of the Estates society in Prussia's key eastern provinces, where the rule of patronage remained entirely unchallenged. It also stemmed, however, from a lack of any experience in autonomous activity, which in turn caused the church – in the Lutheran east, especially – to adopt a policy of 'let's wait and see'. This particular shortcoming meant also that the church even failed to capitalise on the most important consequence of the Revolution, i.e. the separation of church and state brought by both the 'imposed' and the subsequent revised Prussian Constitution.[80] With the right approach, this could have offered tremendous potential for achieving synodal autonomy.

The separation process was hampered considerably by the territorial princes' continuing control of the church, still intact despite all the changes brought about by the revolution. Whilst the Catholic Church – with its inbuilt guarantees of structural autonomy – not only successfully withstood the separation process but also drew certain advantages from it,[81] the Protestant Church was simply drawn more deeply into a dilemma: it was separated from the state, but without achieving genuine independence. It remained dependent upon the helping hand of the King, as *summus episcopus*. After the collapse of the revolution,

however, the King was far from favourably disposed towards
helping the church to set up a synodal structure. On the
contrary: state reaction spread in full force to the church which,
thanks to its innate constitutional weaknesses, suffered even
more severely than the political realm did. The King now
turned his attention towards extending those institutions which
embodied the principle of a state church, abandoning, after a
preliminary period, the presbyterial and synodal counterweights. In 1850, he transformed a department of the Ministry
of Education and Cultural Affairs into the Protestant Supreme
Church Council, an independent authority that was to determine the fate of the Protestant Church in the Old-Prussian
provinces until the subsequent demise of the Prussian state.[82]

The development of the Prussian Protestant Church thus
proceeded at quite a different pace during the aftermath of the
revolution. During the *Vormärz* period (1815-48), it had even
been, on occasions, somewhat ahead of political change, but it
was now lagging hopelessly behind. Since the revolution, the
state had at its disposal a number of parliamentary committees
in the two chambers of the House of Deputies and the House of
Lords, which although set up, from 1849, in the course of three-
class suffrage law, still represented an extra means of forming
Prussian public opinion. They furthermore encouraged the
growth of political parties. The Protestant Church, by contrast,
had no representative bodies that could have acted as a
counterbalance to its own bureaucratic administration. It was
not in any position to involve its employees adequately in the
decisionmaking process, nor was it able to make any 'parliamentary' contribution towards integrating Prussia's provinces. Ecclesiastically, Prussia would long remain trapped by
various forms of provincialism.[83]

It was not until the start of the New Era in 1858 that fresh
attempts were made to re-open the issue of the church's
structure. Guided by the new, moderate conservative Minister
of Education and Cultural Affairs, Bethmann Hollweg,[84] Prince
Regent William ordered that the deadlocked negotiations on
extending the Protestant Church constitution be resumed and,

most notably, that presbyteries be set up along the lines of earlier, stillborn initiatives.[85] Primarily, this was urgently required in the monarchy's eastern provinces which – in contrast to the west – were without ecclesiastical representation and, in effect, had not progressed beyond the level attained in 1816. Simply for the sake of the Prussian Established Church's uniformity, if nothing else, it thus seemed imperative to secure for the eastern provincial churches the same opportunities for presbyterial and synodal development as were available in the west.

But, as was so often the case in nineteenth-century Prussian ecclesiastical history, the road that lay between the plan and its realisation turned out to be longer than anticipated. Presbyteries were set up only slowly, on account of the existing system of patronage. Accordingly, it was quite some time before the *Kreis* synods were finally able to meet.[86] The provincial synods did not meet jointly until 1869,[87] creating the following absurd situation: inhabitants of Brandenburg, Pomerania, East and West Prussia, Posen, Silesia and the province of Saxony were granted universal, secret and equal suffrage for elections to the *Reichstag* of the North German Federation before they could have their own provincial synods or even, in the majority of cases, any proper and functioning church parish councils! Ecclesiastical constitutional development, with all its repercussions upon popular social and political awareness, was almost inconceivably backward when compared with its political counterpart.

The matter was left unresolved until the onset of the *Kulturkampf*.[88] Thanks to the temporary state of alliance between the Prussian government and various liberal opponents of the Catholic Church, an opportunity came about for presbyterial–synodal structures to be extended fairly widely throughout Prussia, although the final result was actually no more than what had been so painstakingly achieved in the two western provinces in 1835. In real terms, this meant that, from 1873, the eastern provinces also enjoyed an ecclesiastical constitution that permitted lay-participation, guaranteeing the electoral principle within the bodies of church representation, from the parishes, to the *Kreis* synods and, finally, the Provincial Synod.[89]

The finishing touch – again, the result of co-operation between the liberal Minister of Education and Cultural Affairs, Falk, and the liberal-conservative President of the Protestant Supreme Church Council, Herrmann – was the summoning of a General Synod comprising all eight provinces of the Old-Prussian Union. Its first meeting was held at the end of 1875, when General Synodal Articles were passed for the eight provinces of the Prussian *Landeskirche*[90].

As Prussia's parliamentary representation, the House of Deputies elected on the basis of a three-class suffrage, began to be overshadowed by the *Reichstag*, the Prussian Protestant Church acquired, for the first time – if one excludes the intermezzo of 1846 – its own state-wide body of representation. In structure, this committee was broadly what the constitutionally-minded thinkers of the time had envisaged, comprising 150 members elected by the Provincial Synods, 30 members appointed by the King, together with the General Superintendents and representatives of the theological faculties of the six old *Landesuniversitäten*. Because, however, it took at least a whole generation before this committee actually came into being, it held little attraction for the up-and-coming forces of the new age. These had long since grown disaffected with the church and, if they were inclined to believe in any parliamentary forms of opinion formation at all, they certainly did not pin any further hopes on the church for this. In Protestant circles – with the exception, perhaps, of one or two areas where the Reformed faith was strong – the view that the church was a concern of pastors and the authorities exclusively had meanwhile become so deeply entrenched that, when it was eventually set up during the 1870s, the synodal system could do little to change things. Ecclesiastical representative bodies were to suffer a perpetual shortage of lay-members drawn from the modern working world.[91]

In consequence, the synods were always several degrees more

conservative than the secular parliaments were. On the right-wing, there were the 'denominationalists', who were still opposed to the *Union* and who dismissed the whole business of constitutionalism as a sign of the Church's secularisation. They comprised roughly one-quarter of the General Synod's membership, and wielded considerable weight in the eastern provinces.[92] Next, there were the supporters of the so-called 'Positive Union', who wished to defend the existing church constitution from what they perceived to be the harmful influences of Liberalism, whilst at the same time tightening up voting qualifications. From the end of the seventies, until 1914, they held a majority in the General Synod, with particularly strong support coming from the civil servants of every province.[93] Allied to them was the so-called 'Middle Party', which in political terms was a broad mixture of Free-Conservatives and National–Liberals and which, during the seventies, was the driving force behind the ecclesiastical constitutional movement. Thereafter, it became the second-largest group in the General Synod, with its main strength located in the urbanised sectors of the Rhine province, the province of Saxony, the Berlin area of Brandenburg and also in parts of East Prussia.[94]

There were hardly any forces to the left of these ecclesiastical parties within the provincial synods, and none at all in the General Synod. The 'Protestant Association', regarded as being liberal, found support only amongst a number of liberal professors, pastors and the circles of the university trained middle class. Because, therefore, it was usually represented on only a very few municipal synods, it was obliged to concentrate upon journalistic output.[95] Friends of Martin Rade and Paul Göhre's 'Christian World', and Friedrich Naumann's supporters, were similarly unrepresented on the General Synod.

In terms of social background, the composition of the General Synod corresponded to its political makeup. At no point prior to 1914 was anyone recruited from the lower classes, and it was even more socially unbalanced with regard to the more elevated strata. The non-clerical members were predominantly drawn from senior echelons of the state bureaucracy and the church authorities, from the squirearchy and the army. One-quarter of them were titled nobles. Of the theological members, more than half were Superintendents and Court Preachers, a further quarter represented the church authorities; the rest were professors of theology, with a handful of ordinary parish pastors.[96]

It was for this reason that the General Synod served not to criticise and oppose the system of territorial rule over the church by secular governors, but rather to support it. If it did occasionally enter into conflict with the Protestant Supreme Church Council, this did not represent any attempt to restrict state power over the church. On the contrary, it was done in order to combat any evident tendencies towards an internal settlement of the Church's grievances.[97] Furthermore, in dealing with the social question – the most important topic of ecclesiastical policy debate throughout the 1890s – the General Synod made no attempt to progress beyond the defensive stance adopted by the Supreme Church Council and discuss, at least, the possible alternatives for resolving social conflict. With the single exception of the socially-conservative former Court Preacher Adolf Stoecker, the General Synod unreservedly supported the sanctions taken by the Supreme Church Council against those clerics favouring a more enlightened social policy.[98]

Here was a particularly striking example of the direct relationship between the church's internal structure and the effect it had upon outside society. Because of its social backwardness and its dependence upon the state and upon the latter's ruling strata, the church was severely hampered from making any progressive contribution towards solving the major problems of the day. To compensate for this, its institutions were, however, highly receptive towards various political movements seeking to balance out the lack of social reform through heightened nationalism. This was the line adopted by the Protestant Church in the war sermons delivered from 1914 onwards.[99]

In light of this development, it was inevitable that the monarchy's collapse was to take a severe toll upon Prussia's Protestant *Landeskirche*. It not only swept away the anachronistic system of territorial rule over the church – which might have meant a step forward – but also removed many of the props and aids with which the state had enabled the church to function in society. It now became appallingly obvious that Prussia's Protestant Church had owed its position much more to borrowed official power than to any innate strength of its own as an institution. Indeed, it had clearly become an area of social backwardness.[100]

The question of how the political changes would be received became increasingly urgent. Was November 1918 to be seen simply as a nasty shock for the world, or as a real opportunity for renewal and reform, and for the church in particular?[101] Comparing the reactions of the Protestant Church in Prussia, with those of other social institutions in the *Reich*, one cannot help noticing that they were especially anti-democratic in tenor.[102] Admittedly, some attempts were made at establishing a new position within the democratic state. Similarly, steps were taken to revise the church constitution, ultimately bringing the formation of a Constituent Assembly, analogous to the National Assembly, though not until two years later. All in all, though, little emerged beyond a makeshift adaptation of the *Landeskirche*'s leadership structures to conform with the new legal situation, i.e. a closure of the constitutional loophole which had been opened up when the monarchy's power as *Summus Episcopus* ended.[103] Thereafter, the highest level of ecclesiastical management fell to a reasonably balanced Church Senate comprising members of the Supreme Church Council, elected synod members, General Superintendents, and heads of provincial synods.[104]

In terms of synod elections, too, far less actually changed than might have been expected, given the frightened reactions at the collapse of the monarchy. Compared with the pre-war period, as far as any shifts in the balance of power within church politics did occur, they were predominantly towards the right. As a result, the share of the mandate held by the 'Middle Party' was reduced to barely one-fifth, whilst the left was unable to achieve more than 10%.[105] The church synods thus remained generally more right-wing than their secular parliamentary counterparts were.

Coupled with this was a strikingly negative attitude, on the part of *Landeskirche* leaders, towards the new Weimar Republican State. The Catholic Church had access to the ruling Weimar Coalition via the *Zentrum* Party and could thus prevent its own anti-democratic elements from coming to the fore. The Protestant Church, however, found it harder to adjust to a Republican political landscape or to compensate for the loss of position which it, particularly, had sustained when the Prussian monarchy fell. Perceiving Weimar democracy as a threat to its own social position, the Protestant Church was now keener than ever before that its policies should safeguard the old social status quo.[106] It was also more determined than before to combat the general secularisation of society. In the opinion of staunch liberal–democrats such as Ernst Troeltsch, the church was in danger of becoming a 'conservative fortress of defence against the revolutionary state'.[107]

This view was to find horrific confirmation during the early 1930s. When, in mid-November 1932, scheduled elections to church parishes and synods were held in the region of the Old-Prussian Union, the NSDAP-affiliated 'German Christians' took one-third of all seats at a single stroke, and up to 50% in the agrarian provinces to the east.[108] Although this matched the National Socialist share of the vote during the *Reichstag* elections held one week earlier, it was more significant since the only other forces of opposition on the church committees were German-Nationalists and right-wing liberals, with almost no leftist groups whatsoever. Unlike the Prussian *Landtag* and the *Reichstag* – where, in every election held during 1932, the National Socialists and German-Nationalists together never gained more than 45% of the seats – the General Synod and the majority of provincial synods of the Protestant Church of the

Old-Prussian Union were almost all composed of representatives of right-wing orientation. The battlefronts against the supporters of Hitler lay far to the right of the Weimar Coalition's position.[109]

The Protestant Church was thus already enduring difficult circumstances as it entered the 'Third *Reich*' and the *Kirchenkampf*. Because it had almost no links whatsoever with modern democracy and, having persistently girded itself against perceived dangers from the left, because it had cut itself off from the latter's resources for democratic opposition to the Nazi state's claim to total power, the church had only a narrow basis of support in the struggle against Nazism. Reinold von Thadden (-Trieglaff), Head of the Pomeranian confessing synods at that time, envisaged tremendous difficulties in mounting any opposition, particularly at the local parish level:

We knew our native area well enough to appreciate the problems that would be caused by any attempt made by a '*fronde*' to go against the official authorities of the State Church or the political powers that lay behind them. Our agrarian province (Pomerania) has always, from the days of 'Old Fritz' onwards, been known for its particular 'devotion' to the State and to the Army . . . Once the 'Third Reich' had arrived, the majority of our congregation completely failed to see any point in resisting the 'will from above' simply because the new sovereignty had cunningly veiled itself in the shining apparel of plans for social reform and caring welfare programmes. The 'Church', however, – known usually to the rural populace only in the form of the local pastor and the squire who was the local patron – seemed to be in league with the forces of reaction utterly opposed to every kind of progress. It was clear that, under such circumstances . . . we could not count on any great sympathy for our resistance movement. At the very beginning, there were not any pockets of organised and trained defence at the local level.[110]

Other members of the Confessing Church have been similarly critical in their judgements of the achievements and shortcomings of church resistance to Hitler. Shortly before his arrest, the theologian Dietrich Bonhoeffer recalled the year 1933:

During those early years, we witnessed a great deal of bravery and sacrifice, but hardly ever found anyone actually prepared to stand up for their beliefs, not even amongst our own ranks. It would be too naive and simplistic to attribute this merely to personal cowardice. The underlying reasons are very different. Throughout our long history, we Germans have had to learn both the need for and the power of obedience. To subjugate all our personal wishes and thoughts to the mission to which we have dedicated ourselves entirely was the meaning and the glory of our existence. We turned our gaze ever upwards . . . It was, inevitably, going to become obvious that the Germans still lacked one basic piece of knowledge: the necessity of free and responsible action, even though this breaks the rules of one's job or goes against one's orders.[111]

This insight into the essential weaknesses of the potential clerical resistance to the 'Third *Reich*' grew only very gradually, as the years passed. Only when the state began flagrantly abusing its power did the heads of the Confessing Church fully appreciate the need to revise the Protestant Official Church's unflinching adherence to authority, if the resistance campaign was to mean anything more than just a one-day protest against various infringements by the state.[112] But this was a problem reaching far beyond the Prussian church, although the latter – with its particularly deep attachment to authoritarian traditions, had greatly helped to blind the broad majority of German Protestants to the dangers from 'above'. The history of the churches' struggle during the 'Third *Reich*' must be viewed equally in a German context as in a Prussian one.

This does not lessen the fact that Prussia's part in the *Kirchenkampf* represented an especially impressive period in the church history of Germany's foremost state. Admittedly, it occurred in marked contrast to all the traditions of the state church within the old authoritarian state, in what was an emphatic departure from outmoded notions of law and order. In the course of its policy of total standardisation (*Gleichschaltung*), the National Socialist regime institutionally 'destroyed' the church of the Old-Prussian Union by stripping it of its administrative organs.[113] At this point, the church found itself obliged to adopt what had hitherto been a thoroughly alien course of action: that of self-help and self-organisation. It was precisely in Prussia that an emergency body of church control was born out of opposition, a leadership structure answerable not to the state, but to the resisting congregation, in the shape of confessing synods and councils of brethren. These mounted especially firm opposition to administrative corruption in the church and – in a series of confessing synods surviving the entire Hitler period – took decisive steps towards reorienting the church.[114]

Thus, the end of Prussia's Protestant Church history was actually marked by the potential for ecclesiastical renewal. Characteristically, the breakthrough came at a time when the state church's notions of authority were in disastrous disarray, and renewal was anything but uncontroversial. That does not detract from its importance, however; on the contrary, because the Confessing Church of the Old-Prussian Union had been so deeply rooted in longstanding Prussian traditions of loyalty to the state, its protest against the perversion of such traditions acquired increased support. Because the Confessing Church had itself grown from a crisis within the old official church and did not simply emerge from a temporary political campaign against a corrupt regime itself in danger of decaying, its wisdom and experience outlived the 'Third *Reich*' against which it had struggled. It bequeathed a legacy of questions relevant to the churches of post-Prussian Germany.[115]

8 ✢ *PRUSSIA: its value today?*

To try to assess the value of Prussia at the present moment is almost as difficult as to pin down the origins of its history. Evaluating Prussia today also requires one to ask discerning questions about the location, date and socio-political background of its genesis; even present-day interest in Prussian history has to be undertaken within a critical and historical framework. The following questions arise: when, where and in what way does Prussia interest us? What sort of people are interested? Not least, which particular aspects are of interest to us today? Such questions may illustrate how the value of an object is somehow related to the situation of the questioner, to the specific circumstances governing his or her perspective. Such questions may show that it is neither immaterial nor accidental when a topic takes on a wider significance within public awareness.

Why should it be that recently, from the early 1980s onwards, there has been renewed interest in Prussia? Why especially now – and not ten years ago – should there be such avid receptiveness for everything published on the subject of Prussian history? Why should there have been mounted, in West Berlin, a major exhibition about Prussia, and why, in the east of the city, should a statue of Frederick the Great, sculpted by Rauch, be re-erected? Are there special reasons for this, transcending day-to-day politics, more than simply a reflection of the usual peaks-and-troughs pattern of political interest?

It is revealing that the writer Sebastian Haffner – who, with his recent publications, has probably done most to revive interest in Prussia – begins his analyses by indicating certain deficits on the political landscape of both German states, and by illustrating how some characteristics of a bygone Prussia are still widely missed today. These are: 'strict Prussian order and truthfulness in the Federal Republic; unsentimental Prussian liberalism and freedom of thought in the German Democratic Republic'.[1]

Unlike the majority of postwar commentators, Haffner does not emphasise nineteenth-century Prussia and its role in helping to unite Germany; instead, he concentrates on eighteenth-century Prussia, the 'raw, rational state'[2] which had grown from the decay of the old *Reich*. 'During its classical period, Prussia was not just the newest state in Europe, it was also the most modern.' It was fascinating for the 'quality of its statehood: its incorruptible administration and independent judiciary, its religious tolerance and enlightened educational system'.[3] This interpretation is not just a set of general points for evaluating a modern state, it is almost a model of Prussia valid for the time of Germany's division into two states. Life is possible if a state fulfills its obligations. It is not necessary for it to concern itself with nationalism in order for it to be meaningful. The value of a state is determined not by its nationality, but by its rationality.[4]

Another widely-read contemporary historian, Bernt Engelmann, has depicted Prussia in much the same light, although his work is characterised by much stronger social criticism. He, too, sees positive features in Prussia before it became a nation-state; he, too, traces certain lines which do not in fact support the idea of Prussia's predominantly 'German' mission. What he finds so fascinating about Prussia is its great ability to absorb immigrants from highly diverse countries, its willingness to help integrate religious refugees, dissidents and settlers of every kind. Accordingly, Engelmann entitles his book *Prussia: Land of Unlimited Possibilities*.[5]

Finally, there is one further current vein of interest in Prussia, similarly concerned with the eighteenth century but examining, in this case, its relationship to the present day. Political scientists such as Martin Greiffenhagen, for instance, use Frederick's

Prussia as a model of comparison with the FRG, identifying certain problems of political development, and posing frank questions as to Prussia's relevance to the present situation:

Cannot eighteenth-century Prussia, a tolerant and enlightened State subject to the rule of law, provide a certain amount of guidance in our own political culture? Is our state not re-enforced by historically recreating that era, those men and those virtues? Can reflecting upon our Prussian ancestry aid our political future? Can we make any use of it, if we call ourselves a 'new' State, unsullied by any shadows from the past.[6]

This illustrates how concern about the FRG's political development can prompt critical analysis of the Prussian past. Because the FRG is a comparatively a-historical state (and the same applies, albeit with certain modifications, to the GDR also), one which is more reliant upon its present-day achievements than upon its past traditions, some consideration of eighteenth-century Prussia can indeed prove useful. Frederick's state, too, was a newcomer amongst the powers of Europe; it, too, was more a product of construction than of organic growth, and was thus unable to fall back on the crucial forces of history for support. Its lack of traditions exposed it to as many hazards as opportunities.

Even disregarding any potential historical parallels, Prussia – prior to becoming a nation-state – appears increasingly attractive to the present-day observer. Above all, Prussia's role in helping to create a modern industrial society is frequently admired; much praise is voiced for the manner in which efficiency was boosted and labour was organised. 'If [Prussian] history has any relevance at all today', stressed a major industrialist, Jürgen Krackow, addressing senior figures from West Germany's financial world, including the president of the Federal Republic, 'then I would say that, amongst other things, it is to be gained from the study of the innovatory role played by the Prussian state during industrialisation.'[7]

Krackow meant that Prussian ministerial officials helped not only to promote industry, but also to develop economic law and to improve social conditions generally. 'The continuing influence of Prussian bureaucratic traditions . . . thoroughly stimulated achievement potential in the industrial society. The industrial entrepreneur shared in the bureaucratic élite's sense of authority and also in their ideals of duty and social responsibility.'[8]

Why these not entirely unfamiliar facts should have come in for emphasis at this particular time becomes apparent later in the same lecture: 'An extremely tense international situation, a world economy suffering from reduced growth, and escalating energy problems will help, in the near future, to create a much simpler form of leadership. We are about to witness the renaissance of a hierarchy and an élite – determined not by social, but by human and qualitative criteria.'[9] This assumption about a new need for authority is allied to a concern that the modern consumer society may lapse into an ideology of laziness:

How many people are there today who make high demands upon themselves, and who are prepared to put in some service? How many people are still aware of or understand the moral value of service? More and more people are becoming prosperous, too comfortable by far to bother themselves with the kind of leadership that involves responsibility, achievement and, of course, risk.[10]

The message is a familiar one, of course: whenever there is increased demand for thrift and achievement, one automatically thinks of Prussia. Wherever there are signs of 'new austerity' (English in original), up spring the typically 'Prussian' virtues of service, asceticism and energy. In testing times, people are fond of recalling Prussia.

But a worsening economic situation would not appear to be the sole reason for renewed interest in Prussia. Shifts in the political balance of power have also contributed. After all, increases in the amount of power wielded by the state awaken either negative or positive associations – according to one's political convictions – with Prussia serving as the epitome of 'The State'. Hence, not only do calls for 'law and order' (English in original) go hand-in-hand with eulogies about Prussian statehood, further development of the socially aware state also prompts consideration of various traditions in official social policy and welfare programmes. Because the state – in defiance of all warnings about the dangers of succumbing to authoritarian tendencies – is becoming ever more closely involved in our daily lives, and because increasingly interventionist measures are expected of it precisely during times of economic stringency, there is growing interest once more in the fundaments of the state, in the scope and limitations of its influence.[11]

The historian Jürgen Kocka – although not referring to Prussia in this particular instance – argues, in the context of society generally, that 'a certain amount of legitimacy' is required by the state in order to fulfill the growing number of tasks it faces.[12] It earns this legitimacy not entirely through its present-day capabilities, but also through its historical roots. Commonsense virtually dictates that one examine the traditions of the past which can help us to survive critical periods today.[13] This becomes all the more valid as supra-national institutions gradually prove themselves to be of only limited efficacy, manifestly disappointing – rather than fulfilling – the expectations vested in them.

Such considerations do not necessarily apply exclusively to Prussia, but they do indicate a possible framework within which certain aspects of Prussian history may be analysed. At risk of exaggerating, one might venture the following assertion: because Europe is obviously no real substitute for a fatherland, and because the German fatherland is no longer a concrete reality, there is growing interest in the traditions of partial states or regions. The FRG and – in a somewhat modified fashion – the GDR are having to abandon their role of being a German stopgap, and in so doing, share certain affinities with earlier state-configurations prior to their becoming fully-fledged nation-states. Because, however, the steps taken towards establishing the foundations of sovereignty coincide with attempts, mentioned above, to bolster the state's position *vis-à-vis* aggressive social forces, it is not surprising that particular interest should be paid to the state with the greatest political prestige in German history: Prussia.

Undoubtedly, this interest may stem from a variety of

motives. Although concerned with the institution of the state, it does not necessarily imply conservative opposition to democratic developments. This is only the case when – as may be occasionally observed – symptoms of political reaction against social reform are also apparent. One might reflect on the fact that Prussia was not in fact an important topic for debate during the turbulent 1960s,[14] but only became current when particular problems emerged during the 1980s. Much of the present-day interest in Prussia is 'post-revolutionary'.

It would, however, be a mistake to over-simplify matters. The East Berlin historian Ingrid Mittenzwei falls into this trap on one occasion in her – otherwise thoroughly subtle and discerning – biography of Frederick, stating: 'There is without doubt a connection between the FRG's shift to the right generally observable today, and the fact that, after all the student unrest of the sixties, there is now great emphasis being given once again to those imaginary 'Prussian virtues'. At the same time, the figure of Prussia's King (Frederick) is being purged of all criticism and raised onto a pedestal again.'[15] Quite apart from the fact that it is the GDR, and not the FRG, that is literally hoisting the great Prussian king back onto a pedestal – in the shape of a giant cavalry monument by Christian Daniel Rauch – this kind of interpretation projects an exclusively conservative attitude onto the revival of interest in Prussia, disregarding all the equally-real, progressive attempts at re-evaluating the subject.[16] Not every aspect of current Federal German debate on Prussia is reactionary.[17]

It must be said, though, that the regression which set in after the over-optimistic expectations of reform during the 1960s and early 1970s did help to create a more sober political climate in which greater consideration is given to the power-political and economic prerequisites of reform policy. As a result, there is renewed interest in a concept which had acquired currency during another phase of Prussian–German history that shared a similar kind of mood. This was the concept of Realpolitik.[18] Associations come to mind, such as the retreat of politically idealistic goals after the collapse of the Frankfurt Parliament, the reduction of liberal hopes for a Prussian state which would preserve at least some of the achievements of 1848. The notion of Prussia as an entity which converted widescale potential for change into concrete necessities of state, subsequently imposing its discipline upon them – is one that can arouse fresh interest at times when the likelihood of comprehensive social reform appears highly remote.

In light of this, it seems indicative that even a book as thoroughly critical of Prussia as that written by the political scientist, Count Christian von Krockow, should open with an analysis of the axioms of Prussian *Realpolitik*. Entitled 'A Prussian Correspondence', Krockow's introductory chapter illustrates the major dispute that took place during the 1850s between Otto von Bismarck and Leopold von Gerlach, concerning the inter-relationship of *Realpolitik* and policy dictated by principles.[19] Here, Prussia is quite clearly noteworthy on account of a particular aspect of its history that might be termed a tightrope walk between revolutionary and reactionary ideals.

In spite of these associations and affinities, the fact remains that 'the bridge between Prussia and the FRG (is) a very narrow one'.[20] Newly-awakened interest in Prussia cannot disguise the fact that Prussia's *raison d'état* was different to that of the *Reich's* western successor, and certainly different to that of the eastern state now encompassing the key area of Prussia's past. Present-day relations between state and society are not as antithetical as they were in Prussia before it became a nation-state, and current intra-German relations are not in any way comparable to Prussia's rivalry with Austria or with the other German powers. Neither of the two modern Germanies is a true successor to the old Prussia.

Nonetheless, this does not prevent them both from competing with one another for the legacy of Prussian history.[21] Reinhart Koselleck's comment about the legacy of Frederick the Great can more or less be applied to the legacy of Prussia as a whole: 'It is as wide-reaching as it remains controversial.'[22] Neither German state can avoid confronting the Prussian past, neither Germany can afford to let the other take sole responsibility for administering that legacy. Controversies about Prussia thus also reflect 'part of both German states' domestic history. Each was and is searching for its own identity. In both cases, the road toward this goal leads through the "Prussian quarter" of history.'[23]

It is more than a 'yearning for Prussia',[24] more than a passing nostalgic whim which thus prevents the ghost of Prussia from being laid to rest. It may be that our current sensitivity towards things Prussian is partly a reaction to the predominance of scholarly disciplines concerned with the present day, but it is nonetheless more than a merely escapist tendency or wish to flee into the past.[25] This new sensitivity towards Prussia more likely expresses growing dissatisfaction with the 'shallowness' of the present, a desire to see it rooted more deeply in the soil of history. Far from indicating a 'flight from Federal Republican reality',[26] it suggests an attempt to safeguard that reality in its entirety, no matter how dubious its constituent elements might be.

This perspective still does not resolve the historian's problems. If it is true that the current growth of interest in history derives, in essence, from insecurity and from a fear of being manipulated; if there is a connection between the desire for a firmer historical grounding and complaints about the symptoms of a 'technocracy without any memory',[27] then there is indeed considerable danger of history being reduced to becoming the mere backdrop to intellectual caprices. Were this to happen, history would lose its critical stance *vis à vis* the present, and would end up only undermining whatever political ideals do still exist.

At this point, at the very latest, there arises the question as to how much this interest in Prussia contributes towards a better understanding of our historical and political identity. Is Prussia simply a random setting within the complex network of contemporary political desires for self-preservation, or can it help us to shore up our fragile age, help us to trace the avenues which led us to our present existence? One thing is certain: even with a highly discriminating approach of this kind, history is still open to abuse, for complete safeguards are not possible. But it does at least suggest one way in which the processes of reflection can be put to good use.

In this respect, it is essential to examine Prussia's historical reality, rather than the images it has projected. If contemporary debate on Prussia were to concentrate solely on consideration of the so-called 'Prussian virtues',[28] then it would have failed to achieve any purpose whatsoever. Virtues such as thrift, love of order, willingness to serve etc., must always be examined only within their specific economic, social and political context. Taken out of context, they may even turn into vices. Not least, they are by no means exclusive to Prussia. Most importantly, that kind of approach would indicate a dubiously narrow angle of political vision if, in the end, only the old German-national evaluations of Prussia were under debate. It would show that Prussia today is worth only as much as German-national ideals care to make of it.[29]

There is not a great deal to be said for interpreting today's wave of interest in Prussia in this particular manner, therefore. Even if one takes seriously the various symptoms of *De-mokratiemüdigkeit* – a weariness with democracy – and considers also certain indications that a crisis of values exists in our modern consumer society, one should still avoid overemphasising the revived discussion of 'Prussian values'. Such discussion is, at any rate, far more subject to democratic constraints than was its disastrous counterpart from the Weimar period.[30]

Analysis of the images projected by Prussia brings us back to the genuine problem of the Prussian state itself, to its extraordinarily abstract quality which makes it so easy, then as now, to light on certain 'fundamentally Prussian' characteristics. That this should be so is an indication of the immense artificiality which Prussia had from the very outset and which constituted its strength, as well as its weakness. Anyone examining 'Prussian virtues' today would do well to remember certain reasons as to why they were so highly-prized. They were crucial because the state of Prussia – lacking any 'natural' basis for territorial, national and social cohesion – was also rather short of alternative sources of integration and strength. With the very best intentions of drawing certain parallels, the same cannot, however, be said of the FRG. Despite its many deficiencies within the field of political culture, the FRG has sufficient internal cohesion and political substance to let thrift, discipline and a sense of duty prevail, without needing to flog to death the Prussian 'model'. A democratic state ultimately has a wider stock of values at its disposal for safeguarding its existence.[31]

Even avoiding a stereotyped image of Prussia, there is still plenty in its history to occupy us today. In the Berlin 'Prussia' exhibition, for instance, close attention is paid to one particular aspect whose significance transcends the narrower context of the Prussian past: the development process of modern German society.[32] The main hall of the exhibition illustrates how Prussia elected to present itself to the public attending the Paris World Exhibition in 1867. It also discusses the path Prussia adopted in order to transform itself from an East Elbian agrarian society into an industrial society, concentrated increasingly within its western provinces. An attempt is also made, with the help of graphical material, to build up a picture of how Prussia 'looked', in terms of both social and economic structure, as an element of the modern world.[33]

No matter how widely opinions may vary as to the value of the 'Prussia' exhibition, the question of Prussia's role in forming modern German society does go some way towards explaining certain phenomena of German economic and social life that are distinct from those of other western European models.[34] If we are to understand modern modes of behaviour, it is essential to know how the social mores of both the influential and the underprivileged were affected by the fact that German industrialisation occurred at a time when Prussia – with its special types of élite – was becoming the leading power in Germany. It is worthwhile examining how the German mentality was influenced by the fact that Germany joined the world of modern industrial societies because of its success in implementing Prussian ideals of authority.

Within this context of Prussia's role in helping to modernise

Germany, there is a further question worth consideration. Which were the Prussian strong points that were fostered in the dual forge of national unification and economic boom, and which were the – equally historical – points which were discarded and which still went on, perhaps, to provide the basis for subsequent innovation? What price did Prussia pay for Germany's so-called Prussian course of development into a major industrial power? Surely, assessing these costs is also part of the weighing-up process we have to attempt today when exploring the limits of technological progress?

In this sense, there is an important juncture of Prussian history to be analysed, a point which has been virtually overlooked in the Hohenzollern state's ascent to German supremacy – the early Stein-Hardenberg reforms.[35] These established standards are worthy of consideration by any society caught between the bonds of tradition and the pressures of modernisation. In particular, such standards of reform may have something to say to a generation made uncertain by modern crises. Whilst today's reforms are often drafted only during times of financial surplus and thus tend to be shelved during periods of economic stringency, Stein and Hardenberg's Prussia enforced a concept of reform completely removing the 'change through growth'/'stagnation' alternatives. Prussia was at that time willing to institute necessary reforms, even during times of material shortage. Chances for social renewal were therefore opened up, not because the resources just happened to be available, but because deliberate priorities had been established.

Undoubtedly, Prussia's reforms, too, were inalienably determined by their time, as were the 'Prussian virtues' of thrift and a sense of duty. But they do at least suggest that there is some justification in preserving an historical awareness of Prussia, no matter how much one may reject the categories of so-called Prussian order.

Notes

Foreword

1 Ingrid Mittenzwei, *Friedrich II von Preussen. Eine Biographie*, Berlin (East) 1979, p. 212, and Karl Dietrich Erdmann, 'Preussens tiefe Spur. Über die geschichtlichen Grundlagen der Bundesrepublik', in *Die Zeit*, 29 Feb. 1980, p. 16.

1. Prussia: when was it?

1 E.g. Sebastian Haffner, *Preussen ohne Legende*, 3rd edn, Hamburg 1979; Bernt Engelmann, *Preussen. Land der unbegrenzten Möglichkeiten*, Munich 1979; *Preussen im Rückblick*, Sonderheft 6 der Zeitschrift 'Geschichte und Gesellschaft', ed. Hans-Jürgen Puhle und Hans-Ulrich Wehler, Göttingen 1980; Dirk Blasius (ed), Preussen in der deutschen Geschichte. Eine Aufsatzsammlung, in *Neue Wissenschaftliche Bibliothek*, Königstein/Taunus 1980; Günter Vogler und Klaus Vetter, *Preussen von den Anfängen bis zur Reichsgründung*, 2nd edn, Berlin (East) 1973; Ingrid Mittenzwei, *Preussen nach dem Siebenjährigen Krieg. Auseinandersetzungen zwischen Bürgertum und Staat um die Wirtschaftspolitik*, Berlin (East) 1979; and *Friedrich II von Preussen. Eine Biographie, ibid.*; Martin Greiffenhagen, *Die Aktualität Preussens. Fragen an die Bundesrepublik*, Frankfurt/Main 1981; Gordon A. Craig, *The End of Prussia*, Wisconsin 1984.

2 Notably Walther Hubatsch, 'Kreuzritterstaat und Hohenzollernmonarchie. Zur Frage der Fortdauer des Deutschen Ordens in Preussen; in *Deutschland und Europa, Festschrift für Hans Rothfels*, ed. Werner Conze, Düsseldorf 1951, pp. 179ff and 198ff.

3 The 'Westinstitut' in Posen is currently compiling a multi-volume history of Germany, with special emphasis on Prussian history.

4 As, for example – with certain reservations – Otto Hintze, in his great anniversary work *Die Hohenzollern und ihr Werk*, Berlin 1915, who remarks, on page 1: 'The State of Prussia is a Hohenzollern creation.' Cf. also Richard Dietrich, *Kleine Geschichte Preussens*, Berlin 1966, p. 9ff. Also, Michael Burleigh: *Prussian Society and the German Order: An Aristocratic Corporation in Crisis, c. 1410–1466*, Cambridge 1984.

5 Otto von Bismarck *Erinnerung und Gedanke, Gesammelte Werke*, vol. 15, p. 197ff. In this edition, chapter 13 appears as chapter 2 of book 2.

6 Otto Hintze ascribes particular importance to this period, above all in his essay 'Kalvinismus und Staatsräson in Brandenburg zu Beginn des 17. Jahrhunderts' (1931), in *Gesammelte Abhandlungen*, ed. Gerhard Oestreich, vol. 3, 2nd edn, Göttingen 1967, p. 255ff.

7 Quoted here from the German edition: *Friedrich der Grosse, Denkwürdigkeiten zur Geschichte des Hauses Brandenburg*, ed. Klaus Forster, München 1963, p. 19.

8 Theodor Fontane, *Die Grafschaft Ruppin*, in *Sämtliche Werke* ed. Edgar Gross, Kurt Schreinert *et al.*, vol. 9, Munich 1960, p. 538.

9 Günter Vogler and Klaus Vetter *Preussen von den Anfängen bis zur Reichsgründung*, begin their short history of Prussia at the year 1701, although there is a foreword on its earlier history. Similarly, Hans-Joachim Schoeps, *Preussen. Geschichte eines Staates*, 8th edn, Berlin 1968, treats history prior to 1701 as prehistory.

10 Cf. Heinrich von Treitschke, *Deutsche Geschichte im neunzehnten Jahrhundert*, 1st edn., Berlin 1879, p. 7. For greater detail, see also chapter 5 above.

11 Hence Leopold von Ranke's emphasis, in the foreword to the new edition of his 'Zwölf Bücher Preussischer Geschichte' (1878): 'The Prussian State is not one of the national powers with long-established justification; it is a power which has grown up in the midst of the latter. Its development has proceeded, step-by-step, in front of the eyes of history,' in *Sämtliche Werke*, vol. 25/26, p. *x*.

12 This date was opted for by Günter Vogler and Klaus Vetter, *Preussen von den Anfängen bis zur Reichsgründung*, whose version ends with the founding of the *Reich*. Schoeps, too virtually completes his history of Prussia at 1871, since he treats everything which followed as nothing more than 'Prussian post-history'.

13 This is obviously the interpretation favoured by Walther Hubatsch: 'ambitious striving by three great Hohenzollern rulers during the seventeenth and eighteenth centuries led to the result that, thereafter, Prussian and Hohenzollern became identical, until – simultaneously with the death of the last holder of the Prussian crown – the Prussian State, too, collapsed'. In *Hohenzollern in der deutschen Geschichte*, Frankfurt/Main and Bonn 1961, p. 23.

14 Cf. also Hagen Schulze, *Otto Braun oder Preussens demokratische Sendung. Eine Biographie*. Frankfurt/Main and Berlin 1977, p. 659ff.

15 Schoeps, *Preussen, Geschichte eines Staates*, pleads emphatically for this date: 'July 20th 1932 – more than any other date – must rightly be said to be the date when, *de facto*, Prussia ceased to exist. On this date, Prussia's post-history ended, and it was followed, several years later, by the end of the German Reich,' p. 296. In contrast, Richard Dietrich, *Kleine Geschichte*

Preussens, p. 259: 'Certainly, Papen's coup did hit Prussia's vital nerve, but it did not finally succomb until Hitler came into power.'

16 See chapter 4, p. 32.

17 The exact text of Law No 46, passed by the Allied Control Commission on 25 Feb. 1947 to dissolve the State of Prussia, may be found in the document collection *Ursachen und Folgen*, edited by Herbert Michaelis and Ernst Schraepler, vol. 23, Berlin (no date), p. 372.

18 Thus, *Die Welt* commented on 'Prussia's End' on 8 Mar. 1947 'On 5th February 1947, Control Council law No 46 meant that the State of Prussia was issued with an official death certificate. This is merely the legal confirmation – death itself occurred some time ago. This funeral is a quiet affair, with an ironic style; Prussia is being buried without any bother, buried in a mass-grave, so to speak.'

19 Sebastian Haffner even likens the victorious Allies' order to dissolve the state of Prussia to 'desecration', *Preussen ohne Legende*, p. 20.

20 Theodor Fontane, 'Der Stechlin', in *Sämtliche Werke*, vol. 8, p. 252ff.

2. Prussia: where was it?

This chapter was published, in an extended version, under the title 'Von der Mark zum Kaiserreich. Ein Staat wächst', in the catalogue for the 'Prussia' Exhibition in Berlin. It is reproduced here with the co-operation of the management of the Berliner Festspiele GmbH.

1 On the origins of statistics in Prussia, see: Otto Behre, *Geschichte der Statistik in Brandenburg-Preussen bis zur Gründung des Königlichen Statistischen Bureaus*, Berlin 1905, esp. p. 130ff.

2 Ranke's summing-up of Prussia's position is particularly apt:

> There was no question here of insularity, such as allowed Great Britain to maintain both a natural dominance over the seas and uninterrupted connections with the continent of Europe; nor was it a case of enjoying a position like that of France, who owes its power to its location – 'twixt the Ocean and the Mediterranean, in the midst of the great cultural lands of Romance and Germanic populations, Spain, Italy, England and Germany; Russia forms a natural link between Europe and Asia, a position from which it derives considerable might; Austria occupies an international geographical position, covering the Alps and turning, across the Adriatic Gulf, towards Italy and the East; it grew mighty by making its goal the West's resistance to Ottoman incursion in the Illyrian Triangle and then wrested the Hungarians from them. How humble was Prussia in comparison, which depended upon just one link between the two German colonies in the East, on the Rivers Oder and Elbe, and beyond the Vistula, a link which it had to rescue from being inundated by the East and upon whose independence its entire territorial position rested! What was characteristic about it was that it was central, increasingly so, between Russia and France and even between England and Austria, whose influence upon the German *Reich* was continually felt in Prussia.

This situation could not have led to any political significance, had it not been for an extraordinary development within domestic resources, coupled with strong yet circumspect conduct of external affairs. Introduction to Book 5 of 'Zwölf Bücher preussischer Geschichte', in *Sämtliche Werke*, vol. 27/8, p. 4.

3   Listed here in accordance with the preamble of contemporary documents.

4   Johann Gustav Droysen, *Geschichte der Preussischen Politik*, 1st edn, 1855, quoting here from the 2nd edn, Leipzig 1868, vol. 1, p. 3f.

5   Most notably, Gerhard Labuda, *Historia Pomorza*, vols. 1 and 2, Posen 1969. Also Bogdan Wachowiak, 'Polnische Forschungen zur Westpommerschen Geschichte im 13.–18. Jahrhundert', in *Greifswald-Stralsunder Jahrbuch*, vol. 12, 1979. p. 226ff. For the German view, cf. Klaus Zernack, 'Preussen als Problem der osteuropäischen Geschichte', in *Nachrichten der Giessener Hochschulgesellschaft*, vol. 34, 1965, p. 259ff.

6   From the diary of the Marchese Lucchesini, entry for 29 May 1781, in *Gespräche Friedrichs des Grossen mit H. de Catt und dem Marchese Lucchesini*, ed. Fritz Bischoff, Leipzig 1885, p. 215.

7   Speech made at the opening of the United Diet on 11 Apr. 1847, in *Der Erst Vereinigte Landtag in Berlin 1847*, ed. Eduard Bleich, Part 1, Berlin 1847, now available as a reprint, Vaduz 1977, p. 22.

8   (Johann Jacobi), *Vier Fragen, beantwortet von einem Ostpreussen*, Mannheim 1841, p. 42f. The original refers not to Prussia's '*Wehrhaftigkeit*' (ability to put up a fight), but to its '*Wahrhaftigkeit*' (truthfulness). As this would not appear to fit in with the line of Jacobi's argument, the necessary amendment was made.

9   Sebastian Haffner, *Preussen ohne Legende*, pp. 72ff.

10 For Prussia's overall development during the first half of the nineteenth century, see Reinhart Koselleck, *Preussen zwischen Reform und Revolution. Allgemeines Landrecht, Verwaltung und soziale Bewegung von 1791 bis 1848*, 2nd edn, Stuttgart 1975. This contains analyses of the development differentials between Prussia's eastern and western provinces (p. 289ff).

3. Prussia: who was it?

1   For the text of the Potsdam Edict of 29 Oct. 1685, see Christian Otto Mylius, *Corpus Constitutionum Marchicarum*, vol. 6, Berlin 1739ff, appendix p. 85ff.

2   More precise figures for Huguenot immigration are given by Martin Philippson, *Der Grosse Kurfurst Friedrich Wilhelm von Brandenburg*, pt. 3: 1660–1688, Berlin 1903, p. 85ff; *Die Hugenotten, 1685–1985*, ed., Rudolf von Thadden and Michelle Magdelaine, Munich 1985.

3   The quotation is given – without any acknowledgement of the source, unfortunately – by Bernt Engelmann in: *Preussen. Land der unbegrenzten Möglichkeiten*, Munich 1979, p. 62.

4 Letter to Georg Friedlaender, dated 5 Apr. 1897, in *Briefe an Georg Friedlaender*, edited by Kurt Schreinert, Heidelberg 1954, p. 310.

5 The statistical data given for the period before the Thirty Years War are only approximations. For further detail, see: Otto Behre, *Geschichte der Statistik in Brandenburg-Preussen bis zur Gründung des Königlichen Statistischen Bureaus*, Berlin 1905, p. 67ff. See also the summary of the growth of the Prussian state under Hohenzollern rule from 1415 in Hans-Joachim Schoeps, *Preussen. Geschichte eines Staates*, 8th edn, Berlin 1968, p. 394ff.

6 Figures for the eighteenth century are very precise. See Otto Behre, *Geschichte der Statistik in Brandenburg-Preussen bis zur Gründung des Königlichen Statistischen Bureaus*, pp. 195 and 202. For Berlin, see *ibid*, p. 205. Cf. also Schoeps, *Preussen. Geschichte eines Staates*, p. 397.

7 Exact data for the population of Prussia at the time of Bismarck's appointment as prime minister are to be found in J.F.G. Eiselen's *Der Preussische Staat. Darstellung seiner geschichtlichen Entwicklung und seiner gegenwärtigen natürlichen, socialen und politischen Verhältnisse*, Berlin 1862, p. 248. Also Schoeps, *Preussen, Geschichte eines Staates*, p. 399, and *Sozialgeschichtliches Arbeitsbuch. Materialien zur Statistik des Kaiserreichs 1870–1914*, ed. Gerd Hohorst, Jürgen Kocka and Gerhard A. Ritter, Munich 1975, p. 42f.

8 Theodor Fontane, *Von Zwanzig bis Dreissig. Autobiographisches*, in *Sämtliche Werke*, edited by Edgar Gross and Kurt Schreinert, vol. 15, Munich 1967, p. 330. The figures given by Fontane are inaccurate. On the eve of the 1848 Revolution, Prussia had about 16,000,000 inhabitants (see *Statistik des Preussischen Staats. Versuch einer Darstellung seiner Grundmacht und Kultur, seiner Verfassung, Regierung und Verwaltung im Lichte der Gegenwart*, Berlin 1845, p. 105ff.) It did not have 24,000,000 until after the annexations under Bismarck (see above). The 4,000,000 it had at the time of Frederick the Great corresponded roughly to the situation in 1763, after the addition of Silesia and before the addition of Western Prussia.

9 Cf. Hans Rosenberg, *Bureaucracy, Aristocracy and Autocracy. The Prussian Experience 1660–1815*, Cambridge/Mass. 1958.

10 On the squirearchy, see Otto Hintze, *Die Hohenzollern und ihr Werk*, p. 55.

11 Cf. Francis L. Carsten, *Die Entstehung Preussens*, Köln and Berlin, pp. 113ff and 123ff, also Hanna Schissler, 'Die Junker. Zur Sozialgeschichte und historischen Bedeuting der agrarischen Elite in Preussen', in *Preussen im Rückblick*, ed. Hans-Jürgen Puhle and Hans-Ulrich Wehler, Göttingen 1980, p. 89ff.

12 Cf. Otto Büsch, *Militärsystem und Sozialleben im alten Preussen 1713–1807. Die Anfänge der sozialen Militisierung der preussisch-deutschen Gesellschaft*, Berlin 1962, p. 75ff.

13 Letter from Fontane dated 9 July 1893 to his daughter Mete, in *Gesammelte Werke*, 2nd ser., vol. 7, p. 281. On the problem of the bourgeois character in Fontane's work, see Kenneth Attwood, *Fontane und das Preussentum*, Berlin 1970, p. 218ff.

14   Cf. Fritz Martiny, *Die Adelsfrage in Preussen vor 1806 als politisches und soziales Problem. Erläutert am Beispiele des kurmärkischen Adels*, Beiheft 35 der Vierteljahresschrift für Sozial- und Wirtschaftsgeschichte, Stuttgart/Berlin 1938. p. 46ff.

15   Gustav Freytag, *Soll und Haben, Roman in sechs Büchern mit einem Nachwort von Hans Mayer*, Munich 1977, p. 330f.

16   Ferdinand Lassalle, *Gesammelte Reden und Schriften*, ed. Eduard Bernstein, vol. 6, Berlin 1919, p. 161.

17   Franz Mehring, *Die Lessing-Legende*, 1st edn, Berlin 1893, now in *Gesammelte Schriften*, ed. Hans Koch, vol. 9, Berlin(East) 1963, p. 8off.

18   August Bebel on 19 Aug. 1904 in Amsterdam, in *Kongress-Protokolle der Zweiten Internationale*, new edn, Glashütten im Taunus 1975, vol. 1, part 6, p. 40.

19   Cf. Hans-Jürgen Puhle, *Agrarische Interessenpolitik und preussischer Konservatismus im Wilhelminischen Reich (1893–1914). Ein Beitrag zur Analyse des Nationalismus in Deutschland am Beispiel des Bundes der Landwirte und der Deutsch-Konservativen Partei*, Bonn-Bad Godesberg 1975, 2nd edn, p. 23ff.

20   Letter to Georg Friedlaender, dated 5 Apr. 1897, in *Briefe an Georg Friedlaender*, p. 310.

21   Cf. amongst others, Ernst Opgenoorth, *'Ausländer' in Brandenburg-Preussen als leitende Beamte und Offiziere 1604–1871*, Würzburg 1967, (Beihefte zum Jahrbuch der Albertus-Universität Königsberg/Preussen, Heft 28), p. 88ff.

22   Theodor Fontane, Der Stechlin, in *Sämtliche Werke*, vol. 8, p. 148f.

4. Prussia: what was it?

1   Hitler's speech in the Garrison Church is included in the 1st volume of Max Domarus, *Hitler. Reden und Proklamationen 1932–1945*, Würzburg 1962, p. 226ff.

2   Reported in *Danziger Allgemeine Zeitung*, 12 Apr. 1932. The title of the article is Hugenberg's Slogan 'Prussia must become Prussian Again'.

3   Oswald Spengler, *Preussentum und Sozialismus*, 2nd edn, Munich 1921, p. 15.

4   Ernst Niekisch, *Entscheidung*, Berlin 1930, p. 48. Similar ideas are also found in the chapter 'Preussen als antiliberale Gründung', in the postwar work 'Deutsche Daseinsverfehlung', now in *Politische Schriften*, 2nd edn, Cologne/Berlin 1966, p. 77ff. Cf. Also Friedrich Kabermann, *Widerstand und Entscheidung eines Deutschen Revolutionärs. Leben und Denken von Ernst Niekisch*, Cologne 1973, p. 93.

5   Cf. Otto Hintze, *Kalvinismus und Staatsräson in Brandenburg zu Beginn des 17. Jahrhunderts*, published first in 1931, now in *Gesammelte Abhandlungen*, ed. Gerhard Oestreich, vol. 3, 2nd edn, Göttingen 1967, p. 255f.

6 For the problem of tolerance in Brandenburg's ecclesiastical policy during the seventeenth century, see: Hugo Landwehr, *Die Kirchenpolitik Friedrich Wilhelms des Grossen Kurfürsten*, Berlin 1894, p. vi, also my book: *Die brandenburgisch-preussischen Hofprediger im 17. und 18. Jahrhundert. Ein Beitrag zur Geschichte der absolutistischen Staatsgesellschaft in Brandenburg-Preussen*, Berlin 1959, p. 130–40.

7 See chapter 5, p. 42.

8 In a review, by Fontane, of Gustav Freytag's *Soll und Haben* of 1855, in *Sämtliche Werke*, vol. 21, 1, p. 225.

9 In contrast to Friedrich Meinecke, who views the two sides of the Prussian state too antithetically: 'Two concepts of state thus co-existed, one humanitarian, the other authoritarian, one newly-created – or at least revised – by the Enlightenment, the other derived from and constantly reaffirmed by the lessons of day-to-day experience . . . The result was a most peculiar and problematical struggle, within Frederick's mind, between the two different concepts of State.' In *Die Idee Staatsräson in der neueren Geschichte*, ed., Walther Hofer, vol 1, Munich 1957, p. 334.

10 The actual words of Tocqueville's comment on Prussia's General Legal Code are; 'Sous cette tête toute moderne nous allons maintenant voir apparaître un corps tout gothique; Frédéric n'a fait que lui ôter ce qui pouvait gêner l'action de son propre pouvoir, et le tout va former un être monstrueux qui semble une transition d'une création à une autre.' In Alexis de Tocqueville, *Oeuvres complètes*, vol 2, i (appendix to *l'Ancien Régime et la Révolution*), Paris 1952, p. 269.

11 There is no evidence, in the works of Mirabeau, of this quotation in this particular form. Schoeps (*Preussen. Geschichte eines Staates*, pp. 98 and 308) offers a comment, made by a Prussian military writer, that is virtually the same.

12 Sebastian Haffner, *Preussen ohne Legende*, p. 76. Immediately before this there is the incorrect Mirabeau quotation.

13 Johann Wolfgang von Goethe, *Aus meinem Leben. Dichtung und Wahrheit*, part 1, book 2, in *Hamburger Ausgabe*, vol. 9, 8th edn, Munich 1978, p. 47.

14 Goethe expresses this idea through the character of a former army doctor in a little-known play *Die Aufgeregten*: 'The Prince thinks the same way as Frederick and Joseph, the two monarchs whom all true Democrats should worship as their saints', in *Goethes Werke*, vol. 5, 8th edn, Munich 1977, p. 202.

15 On the problem of Prussian history as social history, see the recent introduction by Dirk Blasius to his edited volume *Preussen in der deutschen Geschichte*, p. 10ff.

16 These words are supposed to have been spoken originally by King Frederick William III, during an audience in Memel in 1807, according to Max Lenz, *Geschichte der Königlichen Friedrich-Wilhelms-Universität zu Berlin*,

vol 1, Halle 1910, p. 78. Lenz comments: 'Yet one should not seek anything very singular or specific to the King within these words. They expressed a sentiment which, during these very testing weeks, was felt by all the best men in Prussia . . .' (*ibid*). Cf. also Siegfried Kaehler, *Wilhelm von Humboldt und der Staat*, 2nd edn, Göttingen 1963, p. 230. In Humboldt's writings, I have found only the following: 'It has often been said – in the most unmistakeable tones of respect – that the Prussian state is anxious to compensate for its loss of external power by means of internal regeneration; at a time when German literature and even the German language are so endangered, the Prussian state has been regarded as preserving both.' Letter to Chancellor of State Hardenberg, dated 22 June 1810, in *Gesammelte Schriften*, vol. 10, p. 300.

17 The complete quotation runs: 'if Idealism, which in intelligence always seeks the primary factor determining every event that occurs, is truly German, then the whole of Germany most be proud of this State's history. Purely through its intellectual energy, it has twice been re-established in decisive battles for its very existence. Given its location and its extensiveness, the position it occupies is one based not on natural conditions but on its intellectual vigour.' Wilhelm Dilthey, *Die preussischen Jahrbücher*, in *Gesammelte Schriften*, vol. 12, *Zur preussischen Geschichte*, 2nd edn, Göttingen 1960, p. 128.

18 Speech given on 3 Dec. 1850, in: *Gesammelte Werke*, vol. 10, p. 105.

19 Memorandum to Prince of Prussia, September 1853, in *Gesammelte Werke*, vol. 1, p. 375.

20 Cf. the very worthwhile chapter 'Das Reich ohne Idee' in Ernst Niekisch's *Deutsche Daseinsverfehlung* (written in 1945), now in *Politische Schriften*, 2nd edn, Cologne/Berlin 1966, p. 110ff.

21 Recent research has rightly characterised the year 1878 as marking a crucial point in the domestic development of the *Kaiserreich*: the transition to economic protectionism and with it, the renewed move towards political conservatism. Cf. Hans-Ulrich Wehler, *Das Deutsche Kaiserreich 1871–1918*, vol. 9, ed. Joachim Leuschner, 4th edn, Göttingen 1980, pp. 48ff and 100ff. Cf. also Gordon A. Craig, *Deutsche Geschichte 1866–1945. Vom Norddeutschen Bund bis zum Ende des Dritten Reiches*, (German translation), Munich 1980, p. 97ff.

22 Carl Zuckmayer, *Der Hauptmann von Köpenick. Ein deutsches Märchen in drei Akten*, 1st edn, 1931, quoted here from the Fischer paperback edition. Frankfurt/Main 1979, p. 89.

23 See above, chapter 5, p. 67ff.

5. Prussia: how German was it?

1 Hans Joachim Schoeps, *Das war Preussen. Zeugnisse der Jahrhunderte*, Honnef/Rh. 1955, p. 286.

2 Hans Joachim Schoeps, *Preussen. Geschichte eines Staates*, 8th edn, Berlin 1968, p. 300.

3 Schoeps actually states 'that a Germany without Prussia is not worthwhile'. *Ibid.*

4 Heinrich von Treitschke, *Deutsche Geschichte im Neunzehnten Jahrhundert*, 1st edn, Berlin 1879; quoting here from the 6th edn, Berlin 1897.

5 Franz Mehring, *Die Lessing-Legende*, 1st edn, Berlin 1893; now in *Gesammelte Schriften*, vol. 9, ed. Hans Koch, Berlin(East) 1963.

6 Treitschke, *Deutsche Geschichte im Neunzehnten Jahrhundert*, p. 7.

7 Cf. especially Rudolf Vierhaus, *Deutschland im Zeitalter des Absolutismus* (1648–1763), Göttingen 1978, and Karl Otmar Freiherr von Aretin, *Vom Deutschen Reich zum Deutschen Bund*, Göttingen 1980; both volumes are in the series *Deutsche Geschichte*.

8 From a satirical song that was very well-known at the time: 'Wenn unser grosser Friedrich kommt und klopft nur auf die Hosen, dann läuft die ganze Reichsarmee, Panduren und Franzosen' (When our great Frederick comes and simply slaps his breeches, then the entire Reich army, the pandours and the French take to their heels).

9 See above, chapter 3, p. *pp.*

10 Mehring, *Die Lessing-Legende*, p. 82.

11 Stein to the Graf Münster, letter dated 1 Dec. 1812, in: *Freiherr vom Stein. Briefe und amtliche Schriften*, new edn, Walther Hubatsch, vol. 3, Stuttgart 1961, p. 818.

12 Gneisenau to Hardenberg, letter dated 15 May 1814, in *Gneisenau. Ein Leben in Briefen*, ed. Karl Griewank, Leipzig 1939, p. 301.

13 This point was emphasised, with particular reference to Bismarck's initial conception of Prussian politics, by Theodor Schieder in his essay 'Bismarck und Europa', in *Revision des Bismarckbildes. Die Diskussion der deutschen Fachhistoriker 1945–1955 (Wege der Forschung* vol. 285), Darmstadt 1972, p. 257f.

14 Friedrich August Ludwig von der Marwitz. *Ein märkischer Edelmann im Zeitalter der Befreiungskriege*, vol 2: 2, *Politische Schriften und Briefe*, ed. Friedrich Meusel. Berlin 1913, p. 223.

15 *Ibid.*

16 For the consequences of this constitutional deficit with regard to the integration of the state, see above, chapter 2. p. *pp.*

17 Paul A. Pfizer, *Briefwechsel zweier Deutschen*, 1st edn, Stuttgart und Tübingen 1831, 2nd edn revised and extended, *ibid* 1832, quoting here from the new edition by Georg Küntzel. Berlin 1911. The paragraph quoted begins with the words: 'it is a case of granting greater unity not to the Prussian State but to Germany, and if. as I believe. Prussia has to provide a lead in reconstructing Germany, then in my opinion it is essential to prevent Prussia from acquiring undue and harmful predominance. We must do all we can to protect and preserve Germany's federative-republican elements.'

18 *Ibid.*, p. 214.

19 Friedrich Meinecke, *Weltbürgertum und Nationalstaat. Studien zur Genesis des deutschen Nationalstaates*, 1st edn, Munich and Berlin 1907, now in *Werke*, vol. 5, ed. Hans Herzfeld, Munich 1962, p. 288.

20 These discussions must be considered within the context of the German Customs Union, in existence since 1833, which had consequences other than purely trade-political ones. Karl Steinacker shared this view (see note 23). *Die politische und staatsrechtliche Entwicklung Deutschlands durch den Einfluss des Deutschen Zollvereins*, Braunschweig 1844.

21 Von Bülow-Cummerow, *Preussen, seine Verfassung, seine Verwaltung, sein Verhältniss zu Deutschland* (part 1), Berlin 1842, pp. 12 and 8.

22 *Ibid.*, p. 274.

23 Karl Steinacker, *Uber das Verhältniss Preussens zu Deutschland mit Rücksicht auf die Schrift des Herrn v. Bülow-Cummerow*, Braunschweig 1842, p. 33f.

24 *Ibid.*, p. 34.

25 *Ibid.*, p. 39. On the German-Polish problem see the recent collection of essays published by the German-Polish Schoolbook Commission: *Die deutschpolnischen Beziehungen 1831 bis 1848: Vormärz und Völkerfrühling*, Braunschweig 1979.

26 Steinacker, *Uber das Verhältniss Preussens*, p. 36f.

27 Quoted from Ernst Rudolf Huber, *Dokumente zur deutschen Verfassungsgeschichte*, vol. 1, Stuttgart 1961, p. 366.

28 *Ibid.*

29 Cf. Manfred Botzenhart, *Deutscher Parlamentarismus in der Revolutionszeit 1848–1850*, Düsseldorf 1977, pp. 132ff and 193ff.

30 The main champion of a German policy at that time was Prussia's Foreign Secretary Heinrich von Arnim, who was also prepared to accommodate the Poles' nationalist yearnings in the province of Posen.

31 Article written on 31 Aug. 1848, in Theodor Fontane, *Sämtliche Werke*, vol. 19 (*Politik und Geschichte*), Munich 1969 p. 45f.

32 *Ibid.*, p. 46.

33 See above, chapter 2, p. 12ff.

34 Variant of the closing sentence of the memorandum, dated 29 Apr. 1848, in:Johann Gustav Droysen, *Politische Schriften*, ed. Felix Gilbert, Munich and Berlin 1933, p. 135.

35 'Die politische Lage Deutschlands betreffend', written 6 Apr. 1848, in:Johann Gustav Droysen, *Beiträge zur neuesten deutschen Geschichte*, Braunschweig 1849, p. 3.

36 Most notably Johann Jacobi, who in the Prussian National Assembly criticised the decrees passed by the Frankfurt National Assembly concerning the jurisdiction of the *Reich* administrator. For Jacobi's earlier attitude, see above, chapter 2, p. 17.

37 This opportunity was discussed sympathetically by Friedrich Meinecke in chapter 3, book 2 of his work *Weltbürgertum und Nationalstaat*, p. 342ff.

38 Reprinted in Huber, *Dokumente*, p. 385ff.

39 Speech given on 21 Apr. 1849, in: *Gesammelte Werke*, vol. 10, p. 32.

40 Speech given on 6 Sept. 1849, *ibid.*, p. 39.

41 *Ibid.*, p. 40.

42 Even in his memoirs *Gedanken und Erinnerungen*, Bismarck still felt obliged to discuss the 'humiliation' of Olmütz, although he now repressed his earlier attitude of approval. See *Gesammelte Werke*, vol. 15, p. 54ff.

43 Paul de Lagarde, *Deutsche Schriften*, Göttingen 1920, p. 6.

44 Cf. Helmut Böhme, *Deutschlands Weg zur Grossmacht, Studien zum Verhältniss von Wirtschaft und Staat während der Reichsgründungszeit 1848–1881*, 2nd edn, Cologne 1972, p. 57ff.

45 Memorandum dated July 1861, in *Gesammelte Werke*, vol. 3, p. 267.

46 *Ibid.*, p. 269.

47 For an interpretation of the overall context of the memorandum cf. Lothar Gall's recent study *Bismarck. Der Weisse Revolutionär*, Frankfurt/Main and Berlin 1980, p. 211ff. It contains, amongst other things, special emphasis on the interconnection between domestic and external political viewpoints.

48 Cf. Heinrich August Winkler, *Preussischer Liberalismus und deutscher National-staat. Studien zur Geschichte der Deutschen Fortschrittspartei 1861–1866*, Tübingen 1964, p. 16ff.

49 Letter to War Minister von Roon, in *Gesammelte Werke*, vol. 6b, p. 134.

50 Cf. Gerhard Ritter, *Die preussischen Konservativen und Bismarcks Deutsche Politik 1858–1876*, Heidelberg 1913, p. 352ff.

51 For the problem of Prussia's Polish policy, cf. especially Hans-Ulrich Wehler, 'Von den "Reichsfeinden" zur "Reichskristallnacht". Polenpolitik im Deutschen Kaiserreich 1871–1918', in *Krisenherde des Kaiserreichs 1871–1918*, Göttingen 1970, p. 181ff, and Theodor Schieder, *Das Deutsche Kaiserreich von 1871 als Nationalstaat*, Cologne and Opladen 1961, particularly chapters 2 and 3. The *Reichstag* quotation is also taken from here, speech dated 1 Apr. 1871, p. 20.

52 *Ibid.*, pp. 30f and 95ff.

53 Constantin Frantz, *Der Föderalismus als das leitende Prinzip für die sociale, staatliche und internationale Organisation, unter besonderer Bezugnahme auf Deutschland*, Mainz 1879, p. 253.

54 *Ibid.*, p. 275f.

55 Friedrich Naumann, *Demokratie und Kaisertum. Ein Handbuch für innere Politik*, 1st edn, Berlin 1900. Quotation here from the 3rd edn, Berlin 1904, p. 166.

56 Frantz, *Der Föderalismus*, p. 276.

57 A graphic account of this is given by a senior German civil servant in Alsace-Lorraine: 'Our society is so influenced by respect for officers that everyone is determined to make his views and opinions fit in with those held by the military. The civil servant, the professor, the distinguished businessman (*Kommerzienrat*), pay rapt attention to what a Commanding General has to say', Friedrich Curtius, in an article written in December 1913, partially reproduced in my essay 'Friedrich Curtius, Elsass-Lothringen und das Kaiserreich', in: *Das Vergangene und die Geschichte, Festschrift für Reinhard Wittram*, ed. Rudolf von Thadden, Gert von Pistohlkors and Hellmuth Weiss, Göttingen 1972, p. 94.

58 Cf. Fritz Stern, *The Failure of Illiberalism*, London/USA 1972, p. xvii.

59 Cf. notably Michael Stürmer, 'Bismarck's Deutschland als Problem der Forschung', in *Das Kaiserliche Deutschland. Politik und Gesellschaft 1870–1918*, ed. M. Stürmer, Darmstadt 1976, p. 20f.

60 See my essay 'Das liberale Defizit in den Traditionen des deutschen Konservatismus und Nationalismus', in the volume edited by me: *Die Krise des Liberalismus zwischen den Weltkriegen*, Göttingen 1978, p. 65f.

61 August Bebel, *Aus meinem Leben*, part 1, 1st edn, Berlin 1910, quotation here from the 1946 edition, Berlin, p. 145.

62 Speech given by Bethmann Hollweg, on 10 Jan. 1914, to the Prussian Upper Chamber, reproduced in excerpts in: *Das Deutsche Kaiserreich. Ein historisches Lesebuch*, ed. Gerhard A. Ritter, 3rd edn, Göttingen 1977, p. 46.

63 *Ibid.*, p. 47.

64 See above, chapter 4, p. 38–9.

65 Hugo Preuss, *Denkschrift zum Entwurf der künftigen Reichsverfassung vom 3 Jan. 1919*, reproduced in: *Ursachen und Folgen, Vom deutschen Zusammenbruch 1918–1945 bis zur staatlichen Neuordnung Deutschlands in der Gegenwart. Eine Urkunden- und Dokumentensammlung zur Zeitgeschichte*, ed. Herbert Michaelis and Ernst Schraepler, vol. 3, Berlin (no date), p. 426. On the general problem of Prussia's position at the time of the founding of the Weimar Republic, cf. Siegfried Kaehler, 'Das preussisch-deutsche Problem seit der Reichsgründung', in: *Studien zur deutschen Geschichte des 19 und 20 Jahrhunderts*, ed. Walter Bussman, Göttingen 1961, p. 214ff.

66 Cf. Hagen Schulze, *Otto Braun oder Preussens demokratische Sendung. Eine Biographie*, Frankfurt/Main and Berlin 1977, p. 252f.

67 Speech given on 13 Mar. 1919, reproduced in: Paul Hirsch, *Der Weg der Sozialdemokratie zur Macht in Preussen*, Berlin 1929, pp. 225, 228.

68 *Ibid.*, p. 229. Hirsch was also keen to see German Austria included in the new German Republic – in agreement with Ebert and the party leadership.

69 *Ibid.*

70 Otto Braun, *Von Weimar zu Hitler*, 2nd edn, New York 1940, p. 356. For the overall context, see: Schulze, *Otto Braun* p. 254.

71 Cf. Schulze, *Otto Braun*, p. 659ff. This also contains a quotation from the German Nationalist *Deutsche Zeitung* of 10 Mar. 1931, in which Prussia is described as 'the real bulwark of the black and red November system'.

72 Walther Rathenau, *Der neue Staat*, Berlin 1919, p. 24. The latin quotation means 'Whatever insanities are perpetrated by Kings, it is the people who have to carry the can.'

73 Several pages earlier, he says: 'Politically, Prussia never got any further than the methods used by enlightened military despotism; geographically, it never got any further than the River Main.' *Ibid.*, p. 20.

74 *Ibid.*, p. 21.

75 *Ibid.*, p. 22.

76 *Ibid.*, p. 24f.

77 *Ibid.*, p. 25. Characteristically, Schoeps omits this final sentence from his anthology: *Das war Preussen. Zeugnisse der Jahrhunderte*, p. 36.

78 Rathenau, *Der neue Staat*, p. 21.

79 Just how strongly aware Bismarck was of Prussia's supra-national, European dimension has been analysed by Theodor Schieder in his essay 'Bismarck und Europa', p. 255ff. Bismarck himself provides concrete evidence of the ethnic aspects of the matter, in a discussion with the Liberal constitutional lawyer Bluntschli on 30 Apr. 1868: 'The Prussians are a strong mixture of slavonic and germanic elements. This is one of the main reasons why they are so useful to the State. They combine something of the slavs' obedience with the strength and virility of the teutons . . .' (*Gesammelte Werke*, vol. 7, p. 253f).

80 These include writings such as Oswald Spengler's *Preussentum und Sozialismus* (Munich 1920) which helped to prepare the ground for a struggle by anti-democratic Prussianism against the democratic State of Prussia (cf. above, chapter 4, p. 33ff). In his introduction to his volume of collected essays *Preussen in der deutschen Geschichte*, Dirk Blasius comments on this problem as follows: 'Germany's first democracy was hindered from asserting itself not so much by Prussia's actual existence during the 1920s as by Prussia's intellectual and spiritual legacy.' *Loc cit.*, p. 24. Cf. also Johannes Rogalla von Bieberstein, 'Preussen und Preussentum', in: *aus Politik und Zeitgeschichte, Beilage zur Wochenzeitung Das Parlament*, Part 2, 1980, p. 26ff.

81 See above, p. 52.

82 Cf. Schulze, *Otto Braun*, p. 725ff.

83 Prussia's ultimate weakness *vis-à-vis* the *Reich* was also partly due to the split in the SPD, which was arguing in favour of a federalistic solution on account of certain power-related factors, but which favoured a unified state in its basic political beliefs. Cf. Hans-Peter Ehni, *Bollwerk Preussen? Preussen-Regierung, Reich-Länder-Problem und Sozialdemokratie 1928–1932*, Bonn 1975, p. 289f.

84 Laws co-ordinating the *Länder* with the *Reich*, 31 Mar. and 7 Apr. 1933. Cf. Karl Dietrich Bracher, Wolfgang Sauer and Gerhard Schulz, *Die nationalsozialistische Machtergreifung. Studien zur Errichtung des totalitären Herrschaftssystems in Deutschland 1933/34*, 2nd edn, Cologne and Opladen 1962, p. 464ff.

85 See Ger van Roon, *Neuordnung im Widerstand. Der Kreisauer Kreis innerhalb der deutschen Widerstandsbewegung*, Munich 1967, p. 394ff.

86 See Law No. 46 passed by the Allied Control Commission regarding the dissolution of the State of Prussia, dated 25 Feb. 1947, in: *Ursachen und Folgen*, vol. 23, Berlin (no date), p. 372.

6. Prussia: how European was it?

 1 Cf. especially Heinz Gollwitzer, *Europabild und Europagedanke. Beiträge zur deutschen Geistesgeschichte des 18. und 19. Jahrhunderts*, Munich 1951, *passim*.

 2 Particularly impressive is Fernand Braudel's most recent plea for a United States of Europe: 'Il faut réinventer les Etats-Unis d'Europe', in *Le Monde*, 13 Dec. 1983, p. 2.

 3 9 Nov. 1876, in: *Die Grosse Politik der Europäischen Kabinette 1871–1914*, ed. J. Lepsius, A. Mendelsohn-Bartholdy and F. Thimme, vol. 2, Berlin 1922, p. 88.

 4 Cf. above, chapter 5.

 5 Ernst Troeltsch, *Deutscher Geist und Westeuropa. Gesammelte kulturphilosophische Aufsätze und Reden*, ed. Hans Baron, reprint of the Tübingen edition of 1925, Aalen 1966, esp. p. 3ff.

 6 Mark Twain, 'Die schreckliche deutsche Sprache', in: *Zu Fuss durch Europa*, Göttingen 1966. Cf. chapter 14 of Gordon Craig's *Über die Deutschen*, Munich 1982, p. 342ff.

 7 Cf. above, chapter 2.

 8 Cf. Gerhard Oestreich, *Friedrich Wilhelm der Grosse, Kurfürst*. (Reihe: Persönlichkeit und Geschichte, Bd. 65), Göttingen 1971.

 9 Cf. Theodor Schieder, 'Die preussische Königskrönung von 1701 und die politische Ideengeschichte', in *Begegnungen mit der Geschichte*, Göttingen 1962, p. 183ff.

10 Cf. Bruno Schumacher, *Geschichte Ost- und Westpreussens*, 5th edn, Würzburg 1959, p. 215ff.

11 Cf. Sebastian Haffner, *Preussen ohne Legende*, 3rd edn, Hamburg 1979, p. 126.

12 Cf. Theodor Schieder, 'Bismarck und Europa. Ein Beitrag zum Bismarck-Problem', in *Deutschland und Europa, Festschrift für Hans Rothfels*, ed. Werner Conze, Düsseldorf 1951, p. 16f.

13 Letter by Bismarck to Gustav von Alvensleben, dated 5 May 1859, in *Gesammelte Werke*, vol. 14, 1, p. 517.

14 Letter by Bismarck to the envoy Graf v.d. Goltz, dated 24 Dec. 1863, in *Gesammelte Werke* 14, 2, p. 658.

15 Cf. Theodor Schieder, 'Bismarck und Europa', p. 17.

16 On this discussion, mention should be made of the great book on Russia by the Marquis Astolphe de Custine, *La Russie en 1839*, 3rd edn, Paris 1857.

17 Cf. Christiane Mervaud, 'Portraits de Frédéric II dans la correspondance prussienne de Voltaire', in *Voltaire und Deutschland. Quellen und Untersuchungen zur Rezeption der Französischen Aufklärung*, ed. Peter Brockmeier et al., Stuttgart 1979, p. 241ff.

18 Honoré Gabriel de Mirabeau, *De la Monarchie prussienne sous Frédéric le Grand*, vol. 1, London 1788, p. 163.

19 Cf. Stephan Skalweit, 'Der preussische Staat im politischen Denken des ausgehenden 'ancien régime' in Frankreich', in *Moderne Preussische Geschichte (1648–1947). Eine Anthologie*, ed. Otto Büsch and Wolfgang Neugebauer, Berlin 1981, vol. 1, p. 231ff.

20 Letter by Tocqueville to Gobineau, dated 30 July 1856, in *Correspondance d'Alexis de Tocqueville et d'Arthur de Gobineau, Oeuvres Complètes*, ed. J.-P. Mayer, vol. 9, Paris 1959, p. 267.

21 Alexis de Tocqueville, 'L' Ancien Régime et la Révolution,' quoted in *Oeuvres Complètes* ed. J.-P. Mayer, vol. 2, 1, Paris 1952, p. 91. The 'borders of Poland' quotation can be found on p. 92.

22 *Ibid.*, p. 270; the first quotation comes from p. 269.

23 Cf. my speech given at the opening of the 'Prussia' exhibition in Berlin 'Preussen – Ein Weg in die Moderne?', in *Aus Politik und Zeitgeschichte. Beilage zur Wochenzeitung 'Das Parlament'*, part 52–3/1981, p. 6.

24 Cf. Günter Birtsch, 'Zur sozialen und politischen Rolle des deutschen, vornehmlich preussischen Adels am Ende des 18. Jahrhunderts', in *Der Adel vor der Revolution*, ed. Rudolf Vierhaus, Göttingen 1971, p. 77ff.

25 Hence Novalis' enthusiasm in *Die Christenheit oder Europa* (Christianity or Europe), written in 1799, 'They were fine and golden times; Europe was a Christian land, one Christianity inhabited this part of the world shaped by Man; a great community of interest bound together the most remote provinces of this wide spiritual *Reich*.' Quoted in *Schriften*, ed. Richard Samuel *et al.*, vol. 3, Darmstadt 1968, p. 507.

26 Cf. Hans Joachim Schoeps, *Das andere Preussen. Konservative Gestalten und Probleme im Zeitalter Friedrich Wilhelms IV*, 2nd edn, Honnef 1957, pp. 62ff and 131ff.

27 Claude-Henri Comte de Saint-Simon, *De la Réorganisation de la Société Européenne ou de la nécessité et des moyens de rassembler les peuples de l'Europe en un seul corps politique en conservant à chacun son indépendance nationale*, Paris 1814, p.89ff.

28 Leopold von Ranke in the Foreword to the first edition of his *History of Prussia* (1847), quoted here from the edition edited by Willy Andreas, Wiesbaden 1957, vol. 1, p. 47.

29 Georg Wilhelm Friedrich Hegel, 'Vorlesungen über die Philosophie der Geschichte', quoted here in the *Werkausgabe*, vol. 12, Frankfurt/Main, 1970, p. 519.

30 Otto Hintze, *Kalvinismus und Staatsräson in Brandenburg zu Beginn des 17. Jahrhunderts*, published in 1931, now in: *Gesammelte Abhandlungen*, ed. Gerhard Oestreich, vol. 3, 2nd edn, Göttingen 1967, p. 255ff.

31 Cf. Ernst Opgenoorth, *'Ausländer' in Brandenburg-Preussen als leitende Beamte und Offiziere 1604–1871*, Würzburg 1967 (Beihefte zum Jahrbuch der Albertus-Universität Königsberg/Preussen, Part 28), pp. 17f and 88ff.

32 Cf. 'Reformationsjubiläen', ed. Georg Schwaiger, *Zeitschrift für Kirchengeschichte* (?), vol. 93, 1982, part 1.

33 Cf. Rudolf von Thadden, *Die brandenburgisch-preussischen Hofprediger im 17. und 18. Jahrhundert. Ein Beitrag zur Geschichte der absolutistischen Staatsgesellschaft in Brandenburg-Preussen*, Berlin 1959, p. 6off.

34 Cf. Klaus Deppermann, *Der hallische Pietismus und der preussische Staat unter Friedrich III*, (1), Göttingen 1961, pp. 62ff and 172ff.

35 Hegel, 'Vorlesungen über die Philosophie der Geschichte', p. 519f.

36 *Ibid.*

37 Haffner, *Preussen ohne Legende*, p. 125f.

38 Theodor Fontane, *Vor dem Sturm*; *Sämtliche Werke*, ed. Edgar Gross, vol. 1, Munich 1959, p. 24.

39 Bismarck actually said: 'Since the death of Frederick the Great, our policy had either been lacking in clear aims, or else they were ill-chosen or ill-executed; the latter being particularly true of the years between 1786 and 1806, during which our policy began and sadly ended without any plan whatsoever.' Quotation from *Gesammelte Werke*, vol. 15, p. 183.

40 Speech by Bismarck on 6 Feb. 1888, in *ibid*, vol. 13, p. 336.

41 Francois-René de Chateaubriand, *Correspondance générale*, ed. Louis Thomas, 5 vols, Paris 1912ff.

42 This problem was especially evident during the Crimean War. Cf. Siegried A. Kaehler, 'Realpolitik zur Zeit des Krimkrieges. Eine Säkularbetrachtung', in: *Studien zur deutschen Geschichte des 19. und 20. Jahrhunderts. Aufsätze und Vorträge*, ed. Walter Bussmann, Göttingen 1961, p. 128ff.

7. *Prussia: what was its church like?*

1 This chapter is, in substance, much the same as my essay 'Kirche im Schatten des Staates', published in Special Issue Number 6 'Preussen im Rückblick' (eds., Hans-Jürgen Puhle and Hans-Ulrich Wehler) of the journal *Geschichte und Gesellschaft*, Göttingen 1980, p. 146ff. Some modifications have been made: discussion of methodological considerations has been omitted here in favour of a more direct Introduction, enabling the lay reader to grasp more easily the basic problem underlying Prussia's

ecclesiastical history. I have also extended the final paragraph so that some reference can be made to the Church's struggle during Hitler's 'Third *Reich*'. I am grateful to the publishers Vandenhoek and Ruprecht for their kind permission to reproduce the essay here.

2 A good survey of the major lines of development of Protestant Church history in Brandenburg–Prussia is given by Otto Hintze in his essay, first published in 1906 'Die Epochen des evangelischen Kirchenregiments in Preussen', now in Otto Hintze, *Gesammelte Abhandlungen*, ed. Gerhard Oestreich, vol. 2, 2nd edn, Göttingen 1967, p. 56ff.

3 Most notably the Conservative leader, von Kleist-Retzow, who had made several appeals for an improvement of the Protestant Church's position. See the stenographic accounts of sessions held in the (Prussian) Upper Chamber, 18 Mar. and 23 Mar. 1887, *Berichte über die Verhandlungen des Herrenhauses*, pp. 53 and 125ff.

4 Speech made by Bismarck to the Prussian House of Deputies, 21 Apr. 1887, in Bismarck, *Gesammelte Werke*, vol. 13, p. 302.

5 *Ibid.*

6 For this reason, I shall be concentrating upon its history.

7 Otto Dibelius, 'Hundert Jahre Oberkirchenrat', in *Hundert Jahre Evangelischer Oberkirchenrat der Altpreussischen Union 1850-1950*, ed. Oskar Söhngen, Berlin 1950, p. 7ff.

8 For the development of authority over the Church at the time of the Reformation in Prussia, see Heinrich von Mühler, *Geschichte der evangelischen Kirchenverfassung in der Mark Brandenburg*, Weimar 1846, p. 47ff.

9 As opposed to Francis L. Carsten, *Die Entstehung Preussens*, Cologne/Berlin 1968, p. 136, who is of the opinion that the Reformation did not increase the Princes' power.

10 This topic has tended to receive scant attention, e.g. in Otto Hintze, *Die Hohenzollern und ihr Werk*, Berlin 1915, more recently published in Moers, 1979, p. 113.

11 This was the case in almost all Protestant territories, with the exception of Württemberg. In the *Reichstag*, however, the clergy continued to be represented within the two upper *Curiae*.

12 During the sixteenth century, there were still certain counterweights in the shape of the fronts formed by denominational sectarianism, which helped to prevent the Church's contours from becoming too blurred. Matters developed differently within the Catholic sphere.

13 Cf. Paul Drews, *Der evangelische Geistliche in der deutschen Vergangenheit, Monographien zur deutschen Kulturgeschichte*, vol. 12, Jena 1905, p. 16ff.

14 Cf. Karl Holl, 'Die Bedeutung der grossen Kriege für das religiöse und kirchliche Leben innerhalb des deutschen Protestantismus' (1917), in Karl Holl, *Gesammelte Aufsätze zur Kirchengeschichte*, part 3, Tübingen 1928, p. 346.

15 Daniel Ernst Jablonski, 'Betrachtungen über das Schreiben des Herrn Bonnet wegen der englischen Liturgie und Kirchenverfassung, vom 27 Apr. 1711,' in *Darlegung der im vorigen Jahrhundert wegen Einführung der englischen Kirchenverfassung in Preussen gepflogenen Unterhandlungen, urkundlich belegt mit Briefen von dem Hofprediger Jablonski*, Leipzig 1842, p. 85.

16 The state's advantage over the Church had left a lasting impression upon the Prussians, see above, p. 87.

17 Cf. Otto Hintze, 'Kalvinismus und Staatsräson in Brandenburg zu Beginn des 17. Jahrhunderts' (1931), in Otto Hintze, *Gesammelte Abhandlungen*, vol. 3, p. 255f.

18 Otto Hintze, 'Die Epochen des evangelischen Kirchenregiments in Preussen', p. 70ff.

19 Rudolf von Thadden, *Die brandenburgisch-preussischen Hofprediger im 17. und 18. Jahrhundert. Ein Beitrag zur Geschichte der absolutistischen Staatsgesellschaft in Brandenburg-Preussen*, Berlin 1959, p. 142.

20 Such as the Court Chaplain Johann Bergius, *Apostolische Regell, wie man in Religions-Sachen recht richten solle*, Elbing 1641.

21 On the problem of tolerance in Brandenburg's ecclesiastical policy during the seventeenth century, see Hugo Landwehr, *Die Kirchenpolitik Friedrich Wilhelms des Grossen Kurfürsten*, Berlin 1894, p. 6 and also my work on the Court Preachers (see note 19), pp. 130ff and 140.

22 For instance, Helmut Erbe, *Die Hugenotten in Deutschland*, Essen 1937.

23 On the problem of pietism, see the still unsurpassed study by Ernst Troeltsch, *Leibnitz und die Anfänge des Pietismus* (1902), in *ibid.*, *Gesammelte Schriften*, vol. 4, Tübingen 1925, p. 488ff, esp. 514ff.

24 See Klaus Deppermann, *Der hallische Pietismus und der preussische Staat unter Friedrich III* (1), Göttingen 1961, pp. 62ff and 141ff.

25 Essential reading on this is Carl Hinrichs, *Preussentum und Pietismus. Der Pietismus in Brandenburg-Preussen als religiös-soziale Reformbewegung*, Göttingen 1971, esp. pp. 174ff and 301ff.

26 Cf. Günter Vogler and Klaus Vetter, *Preussen. Von den Anfängen bis zur Reichsgründung*, Berlin (East) 1973, p. 76.

27 On this, Ernst Troeltsch, 'Die Soziallehren der christlichen Kirchen und Gruppen', in *ibid.*, *Gesammelte Schriften*, vol. 1, Tübingen 1923, p. 827ff.

28 Not even the Huguenots were permitted to establish synods in Prussia. At parish level they had presbyteries and, above these, a so-called *Consistoire Supérieur*.

29 Otto Hintze summed this up in his essay on the various epochs of Protestant church administration in Prussia ('Die Epochen des evangelischen Kirchenregiments in Preussen', p. 73) as follows: 'Spiritual and temporal rule were now no longer dual functions of one and the same Christian body, united by faith and denomination. Spiritual rule now appeared to be an attribute of temporal rule, an accessory of the state's

authority. Only now did the church become the Official Church, fully subordinate to the state.'

30 The process of this development is discussed from the point of view of the way in which offices were accumulated, in my study of the Court preachers, *Die brandenburgisch – preussischen Hofprediger*; p. 45ff.

31 Cf. Karl Aner, *Die Theologie der Lessingzeit*, Halle 1929 and Hildesheim 1964, pp. 14ff and 61ff.

32 August Friedrich Wilhelm Sacks *Lebensbeschreibung nebst einigen von ihm hinterlassenen Briefen und Schriften*, ed. by his son Friedrich Samuel Gottfried Sack, vol. 2, Berlin 1789, p. 89.

33 Especially Paul Schwartz, *Der erste Kulturkampf in Preussen um Kirche und Schule (1788–1798)*, Berlin 1925.

34 The Edict is reproduced in Christian Otto Mylius, *Novum Corpus Constitutionum Prussico-Brandenburgicarum*, vol. 8, Berlin 1791, p. 2175.

35 See Ernst Rudolf Huber, *Deutsche Verfassungsgeschichte seit 1789*, vol. 1, 2nd edn, Stuttgart 1967, p. 394.

36 Since 1750, there had been a Lutheran Upper Consistory for the whole state, superior to the individual *Provinz* consistories, but not vested with any clerical jurisdiction, which had been removed from the latter in 1748. It did, however, always have one Reformed Court preacher as a member.

37 Above all, a 'most humble memorandum', submitted by the Court preacher and Councillor of the Upper Consistory, Friedrich Samuel Gottfried Sack, to the Reformed Minister of Clerical Affairs, dated 26 Aug. 1788, discussed in my study of the Court Preachers, *Die brandenburgisch – preussischen Hofprediger*, p. 125f.

38 The five Councillors' petition was rejected, with the comment 'insubordination'. *Ibid.*

39 There has been no recent research into this subject. Reinhart Koselleck's work *Preussen zwischen Reform und Revolution*, 2nd edn, Stuttgart 1975, p. 163ff, makes no reference to the clerical and ecclesiastical area of the Stein–Hardenberg reforms. One therefore must rely upon sections of older works.

40 The part of the Prussian Legal Code relating to the church is reproduced in Ernst Rudolf and Wolfgang Huber, *Staat und Kirche im 19. und 20. Jahrhundert*, vol. 2, Berlin 1976, p. 3ff.

41 For Schleiermacher's contribution to the reorganisation of the Church in Prussia, see Martin Honecker, *Schleiermacher und die Reform der Kirchenverfassung*, in *Festschrift für Ernst Rudolf Huber*, Göttingen 1973, p. 57ff.

42 Schleiermacher's 'Entwurf einer neuen Kirchenordnung der preussischen Monarchie' of September 1808 was published in *Doves Zeitschrift für Kirchenrecht*, Jg. 1861, p. 327ff.

43 *Ibid.*

44 See Gerhard Ritter, *Stein. Eine politische Biographie*, Stuttgart 1931, p. 456f.

45 *Publikandum die veränderte Verfassung der obersten Staatsbehörden betreffend vom 16 Dez. 1808*, published in excerpt form in Huber, *Staat und Kirche*, vol, 1, p. 55.

46 For an interpretation of this process, see Huber, *Deutsche Verfassungsgeschichte*, vol. 1, p. 461. It is emphasised here how this reform was intended only as a transitional measure prior to a more comprehensive reorganisation of the church.

47 Since the Prussian Legal Code was enacted, there was parity between the three major Christian communities. See *ibid.*, p. 397f.

48 The text of the Edict of 30 Oct. 1810 is in Huber, *Staat und Kirche*, vol. 1, p. 58. [Translator's note: *Reichsdeputationshauptschluss* = A resolution by a committee of the Imperial Diet, mediatizing and secularizing almost all ecclesiastical principalities.]

49 *Verordnung wegen verbesserter Einrichtung der Provinzial-Behörden vom 30. Apr. 1815, ibid.*, p. 119f.

50 Cf. especially Richard Wilhelm Dove, 'Uber Synoden in der evangelischen Landeskirche Preussens', in *Doves Zeitschrift für Kirchenrecht*, Jg.2, 1862, pp. 131ff and Jg. 4, 1864, p. 131ff.

51 Useful in understanding this position is Fritz Fischer's *Ludwig Nicolovius. Rokoko-Reform-Restauration*, Stuttgart 1939, particularly pp. 354, 365ff, 410ff and 433ff.

52 *Kabinettsordre betreffend die Verbesserung der evangelischen Kirchenverfassung in Preussen vom 27.5.1816*, reproduced in extracts in Huber, *Staat und Kirche*, vol. 1, p. 574ff. This Cabinet Order was in part the result of the reports submitted, a year earlier, by a clerical commission set up to consider the Church's constitution.

53 *Ibid.*, p. 576.

54 *Ibid.*, p. 575.

55 Schleiermacher referred harshly to the proposed General Superintendents as 'spiritual prefects'; see Fritz Fischer, *Ludwig Nicolovius, loc cit.*, p. 366 and 412.

56 See Erich Foerster, *Die Entstehung der preussischen Landeskirche unter der Regierung König Friedrich Wilhelms III*, vol. 2, Tübingen 1907, pp. 3f and 7ff. For comparison: in the political sphere, *Provinz* estates were not set up until 1823, *Kreis* diets not until 1825. Institutional changes to *Land* parishes were not made until Frederick William IV's rule.

57 *Ibid.*, pp. 9f and 23ff.

58 *Ibid.*, p. 15.

59 Cf. Gerhard Ruhbach, *Die Religionspolitik Friedrich Wilhelms III von Preussen*, in: *Bleibendes im Wandel der Kirchengeschichte. Festschrift für Hans Freiherrn von Campenhausen*, ed. Bernd Moeller and Gerhard Ruhbach, Tübingen 1972, p. 307ff.

60 *Ibid.*, p. 323ff and Foerster, *Die Entstehung der preussischen Landeskirche*, p. 55ff.

61 See Walter Göbell, *Die rheinisch-westfälische Kirchenordnung vom 5 März 1835. Ihre geschichtliche Entwicklung und ihr theologischer Gehalt*, 2 vols., Duisburg 1948ff, also the text of the *Kirchenordnung, vol. 1, p. 173ff.*

62 The Rhenish–Westphalian Church Regulation did not abolish the *Provinz* consistories, but complemented them with synods. The latter also embodied the state's rights of supervision over the Church.

63 Cf. Th. Hoffmann, *Die Einführung der Union in Preussen und die durch die Union veranlasste Separation der Altlutheraner*, Berlin 1903, and Wilhelm Iwan, *Die Altlutheranische Auswanderung um die Mitte des 19. Jahrhunderts*, Ludwigsburg 1943.

64 Cabinet Order of 2 Sept. 1837, reprinted in: Foerster, *Die Entstehung der preussischen Landskirche*, vol. 2, p. 309.

65 Important sections on the Pietist Awakening movement are contained in the excellent study by Robert M. Bigler, *The Politics of German Protestantism. The Rise of the Protestant Church Elite in Prussia, 1815–1848*, Berkeley 1972, p. 125ff.

66 There is still a lack of recent studies of Frederick William IV's religiosity and ecclesiastical principles; cf. however Huber, *Deutsche Verfassungsgeschichte*, vol. 2, p. 275f and Johannes Heckel, 'Ein Kirchenverfassungsentwurf Friedrich Wilhelms IV von 1847', in *Das blinde, undeutliche Wort 'Kirche', Gesammelte Aufsätze*, ed. Siegfried Grundmann, Cologne/Graz, 1964, p. 434ff.

67 For instance, Theodor von Schön, *Woher und Wohin?* Strassburg 1842, and Johann Jacobi, *Vier Fragen beantwortet von einem Ostpreussen*, Mannheim 1841.

68 A different line is pursued here by Bruno Bauer, *Die evangelische Landeskirche Preussens und die Wissenschaft*, 2nd edn, Leipzig 1840, who – with regard to room for free manoeuvre – set greater store by state policy than by church developments.

69 See Huber, *Staat und Kirche*, vol. 1, p. 610ff, which also gives the exact text of the Regulation of 27 June 1845.

70 The *Provinz* Estates also convened a year later than the *Provinz* synods, i.e. 1845. On the United Diet, see Ernst Rudolf Huber, *Deutsche Verfassungsgeschichte*, vol. 2, p. 491ff.

71 Cf. Fritz Fischer, *Moritz August von Bethmann-Hollweg und der Protestantismus*, Berlin 1937, p. 174, and also Hans Rosenberg, 'Theologischer Rationalismus und vormärzlicher Vulgärliberalismus', in *Historische Zeitschrift*, 141/1930, p. 497ff.

72 Taken from the King's Convening Decree, in *Verhandlungen der evangelischen General-Synode zu Berlin vom 2. Juni bis zum 29. August 1846*, Berlin 1846, p. 1.

73 Some of the holders of state offices also had other overlaps, though not the clergy, who were not represented in the United Diet.

74 The exact text can be found in *Verhandlungen der evangelischen General-Synode*, p. 118f. As far as the setting-up of presbyteries was concerned, reservations existed on account of the rights of patronage that were in operation.

75 Only on one point did the King meet the synods' wishes: in the setting-up of an Upper Consistory for the entire state. It was brought into being by Decree on 28 Jan. 1848, but dissolved within three months because of the subsequent March Revolution. See Huber, *Staat und Kirche*, vol. 1, p. 625ff.

76 There is still a shortage of works on the history of the Protestant Church during the revolutionary year 1848. However, there is Ernst Schubert, *Die evangelische Predigt im Revolutionsjahr 1848*, in *Studien zur Geschichte des neueren Protestantismus*, Heft 8, Giessen 1913, and Walter Delius, *Die evangelische Kirche und die Revolution 1848*, Berlin 1948.

77 On this, Günter Brakelmann, *Kirche und Sozialismus im 19. Jahrhundert*, Witten 1966, especially p. 35ff, and William O. Shanahan, *Der deutsche Protestantismus vor der sozialen Frage 1815–1871*, German translation, Munich 1962, p. 243ff.

78 It would be a worthwhile exercise pursuing the regional history of the Church in 1848 in greater detail. For the Rhineland and Westphalia, see Walter Göbell, *Die rheinisch – westfälische Kirchenordnung*, p. 246f (vol. 1).

79 *Die Verhandlungen der Wittenberger Versammlung für die Gründung eines Deutschen Evangelischen Kirchenbundes im September 1848*, ed. Kling, Berlin 1848, p. 128.

80 The corresponding Article 15 of the revised Constitution of 31 Jan. 1850 (= Article 12 of the Imposed Constitution of 5 Dec. 1848) states: 'The Protestant and the Roman Catholic Church, like any other religious society, organises and administers its affairs independently . . .' Huber, *Staat und Kirche*, vol. 2, p. 36f.

81 For this, A. L. Richter, 'Die Entwicklung des Verhältnisses zwischen dem Staate und der katholischen Kirche in Preussen seit der Verfassungsurkunde vom 5. Dec. 1848', in: *Doves Zeitschrift für Kirchenrecht*, Jg. 1, 1861, p. 100ff.

82 The corresponding Decree by the King, dated 29 June 1850 (reprinted in: Huber, *Staat und Kirche*, vol. 2, p. 315ff) contained, in addition, a passage concerning the principles of a Parish Regulation, which – in the subsequent years of reaction – failed to be implemented.

83 E. R. Huber refers, in this context, to 'ecclesiastical late-absolutism': *Deutsche Verfassungsgeschichte*, vol. 4, p. 837.

84 Unfortunately, the abovementioned study of Bethmann-Hollweg by Fritz Fischer does not cover this period. A second volume failed to appear.

85 *Erlass des Prinzregenten Wilhelm an den Kultusminister von Bethmann-Hollweg betreffend die Fortbildung der evangelischen Kichenverfassung in den östlichen Provinzen der Monarchie vom 27.2.1860*, reproduced in extracts in Huber, *Staat und Kirche*, vol. 2 p. 333f.

86 Decree for the Province of Prussia, dated 5 June 1861; for the Province of Posen, dated 5 Apr. 1862; for the Province of Pomerania, dated 21 June 1862; for the Provinces of Brandenburg, Silesia and Saxony, dated 13 June 1864; see Huber, *Deutsche Verfassungsgeschichte*, vol. 4, p. 846.

87 Decree of 5 June 1869, reprinted in Huber, *Staat und Kirche*, vol. 2, p. 335. The areas annexed during 1864/6 retained their own churches; they were not incorporated into the Prussian Official Church.

88 An important study of the long-neglected topic of Protestant Church policy at the time of the founding of the Reich and during the *Kulturkampf* was published fairly recently: Gerhard Besier, *Preussische Kirchenpolitik in der Bismarckära. Die Diskussion in Staat und evangelischer Kirche um eine Neuordnung der kirchlichen Verhältnisse zwischen 1866 und 1872*, Berlin 1980. In addition, chapter 10 of the biography by Erich Foerster, *Adalbert Falk*, Gotha 1927, p. 302ff, is still useful.

89 Parish and Synodal Regulation of 10 Sept. 1873, reproduced in Huber, *Staat und Kirche*, vol. 2, p. 933ff.

90 General Synod Regulation for the Protestant Church of the Eight Original Provinces of the Monarchy, dated 20 Jan. 1876, *ibid.*, p. 944ff.

91 Cf. Huber, *Deutsche Verfassungsgeschichte*, vol. 4, p. 852f. The General Synod's appeal was reduced also by the fact that – although it was supposed to meet only once every six years – it actually did so every three years.

92 Cf. the excellent work by Klaus Erich Pollmann, *Landesherrliches Kirchenregiment und soziale Frage. Der evangelische Oberkirchenrat der altpreussischen Landeskirche und die sozialpolitische Bewegung der Geistlichen nach 1890*, Berlin 1973, particularly pp. 46f and 57ff.

93 *Ibid.*, p. 62f. They included the Court Preachers Kögel and Stoecker, who played prominent roles.

94 *Ibid.*, p. 60f. The 'Middle Party' was officially titled the '*Landeskirchliche evangelische Vereinigung*'. Its most prominent representative was the president of the Protestant Supreme Church Council, Herrmann.

95 Its most important organ was the *Deutsche Protestantenblatt*, which appeared, from 1868 onwards, in Bremen.

96 Cf. Klaus Erich Pollmann, *Landesherrliches Kirchenregiment* p. 51f.

97 *Ibid.*, p. 43f. The same was also true of the behaviour of the provincial synods towards the provincial consistories.

98 For the attitude of the General Synod of 1897 towards the Decree issued by the Supreme Church Council on 16 Dec. 1895, see: *ibid.*, p. 226ff. The text of the Decree, together with an excerpt from the synodal debate can be found in Günter Brakelmann, *Kirche, soziale Frage und Sozialismus*, vol. 1: *Kirchenleitungen und Synoden über soziale Frage und Sozialismus 1871–1914*, Gütersloh 1977, pp. 189ff and 193ff.

99 Cf. Wilhelm Pressel, *Die Kriegspredigt 1914–1918 in der evangelischen Kirche Deutschlands*, Göttingen 1967, esp. pp. 15ff, 75ff, and 346ff. Also

Reinhard Wittram, *Kirche und Nationalismus in der Geschichte des deutschen Protestantismus im 19. Jahrhundert*, in *ibid. Das Nationale als europäisches Problem*, Göttingen 1954, p. 109ff.

100 In many ways, this also applied to the other Protestant states, but it was particularly true of Prussia on account of the Monarchy's extreme power.

101 See Martin Greschat, *Der deutsche Protestantismus im Revolutionsjahr 1918/19, Bd. II der Studienbücher zur kirchlichen Zeitgeschichte*, Witten 1974, p. 9ff.

102 This was ably demonstrated by Jochen Jacke in his study *Kirche zwischen Monarchie und Republik. Der deutsche Protestantismus nach dem Zusammenbruch von 1918*, Hamburg 1976, esp. p. 328ff. Less detailed a treatment is that by Claus Motschmann, *Evangelische Kirche und preussischer Staat in den Anfängen der Weimarer Republik*, Hamburg 1969.

103 Jochen Jacke, *Kirche zwischen Monarchie und Republik*, p. 298ff.

104 *Ibid.*, p. 265ff.

105 These figures apply to the elections to the Constituent Assembly of 1921. Account should be taken of the general shift towards the right visible throughout Germany from 1920 onwards.

106 Above all, there was not permitted to be any widening of powers at parish level. This was intended – in East Elbian circles, at any rate – to prevent the church from developing any forms of democratic co-responsibility.

107 Ernst Troeltsch, *Spektatorbriefe*, ed. Hans Baron, Tübingen 1924, p. 80. This statement was made whilst Troeltsch was working as Under Secretary in the Prussian Ministry of Education.

108 See Jonathan R.C. Wright, '*Uber den Parteien'. Die politische Haltung der evangelischen Kirchenführer 1918–1933*, Göttingen 1977, p. 161f; Klaus Scholder, *Die Kirchen und das Dritte Reich*, vol. 1: *Vorgeschichte und Zeit der Illusionen 1918–1934*, Frankfurt/Main, Berlin, Vienna 1977, p. 272f.

109 This must be said in order to correct the rather misleading picture given by both Wright and Scholder, who fail to put the '*Deutsche Christen*''s share of the vote within a sufficient context. They do, however, make an important distinction between the East Elbian and the western provinces, stressing that in the latter – with its presbyterial–synodal traditions – the '*Deutsche Christen*' were not able to obtain as large a share of the vote as they did in the eastern regions.

110 Reinhold von Thadden, *Auf verlorenem Posten? Ein Laie erlebt den evangelischen Kirchenkampf in Hitlerdeutschland*. Tübingen 1948, p. 78ff.

111 Dietrich Bonhoeffer, *Widerstand und Ergebung. Briefe und Aufzeichnungen aus der Haft*, ed. Eberhard Bethge, new edn, Munich 1970, p. 14.

112 This is particularly emphasised by Ernst Wolf, *Zum Verhältnis der politischen und moralischen Motive in der deutschen Widerstandsbewegung*, in *Der deutsche Widerstand gegen Hitler. Vier historisch-kritische Studien ...*, ed. Walter Schmitthenner und Hans Buchheim, Cologne/Berlin 1966, pp. 219 and 230.

113 The relevant sources are to be found in the collection: *Dokumente zur*

Kirchenpolitik des Dritten Reiches, vol. 1 (*Das Jahr 1933*), prepared by Carsten Nicolaisen, Munich 1971, p. 67ff. Further: Oskar Söhngen, *Die Reaktion der 'amtlichen' Kirche auf die Einsetzung eines Staatskommissars durch den nationalsozialistischen Staat*, in *Zur Geschichte des Kirchenkampfes. Gesammelte Aufsätze II*, ed. Heinz Brunotte, Göttingen 1971, p. 35ff.

114 Cf. above all Wilhelm Niesel, *Kirche unter dem Wort. Der Kampf der Bekennenden Kirche der altpreussischen Union 1933–1945*, Göttingen 1978, pp. 16ff and 28ff. This also gives a description of how specifically Prussian Confessional synods and councils of brethren were set up in parallel with those for the *Reich*.

115 Cf. my essay on 'Dietrich Bonhoeffer und der deutsche Nachkriegsprotestantismus', in *Kirchen in der Nachkriegszeit. Vier zeitgeschichtliche Beiträge von Arnim Boyens, Martin Greschat, Rudolf von Thadden, Paolo Pombeni*, Göttingen 1979, p. 125ff.

8. Prussia: its value today?

1 Sebastian Haffner, *Preussen ohne Legende*, 3rd edn, Hamburg 1979, p. 21.

2 *Ibid.*, p. 72ff.

3 *Ibid.*, p. 21.

4 Haffner refers to Prussia as a 'rational-state', rather than a 'national-state', *ibid.*, p. 128.

5 Bernt Engelmann, *Preussen. Land der unbegrenzten Möglichkeiten*, Munich, 1979, p. 7.

6 Martin Greiffenhagen, *Die Aktualität Preussens. Fragen an die Bundesrepublik*, Frankfurt/Main 1981, p. 15f.

7 Jürgen Krackow, 'Preussen. – Ein kritischer Massstab für unsere Industriegesellschaft?' in *Das Bremer Tabak-Kollegium*. III. Zusammenkunft am 8. Juni 1980 im Schloss Bellevue, Berlin, p. 21. Part of this lecture was also reprinted in the *Frankfurter Allgemeine Zeitung* of 2 Aug. 1980, under the title 'What We Can Learn from Prussia. A Plea for a Return to Old Virtues and Values'.

8 *Ibid.*, p. 24. Cf. Gustav Stolper, *Deutsche Wirtschaft seit 1870*, 2nd enlarged edn, Tübingen 1966, p. 45ff.

9 Krackow, 'Preussen', p. 29.

10 *Ibid.*

11 Examples of increased calls for state intervention are found, not least, in the area of educational policy, albeit with varying party-political approaches. Cf. my essay: *Institution und politisches Handeln. Zur Frage des Handlungsspielraums eigenständiger institutionen* (Göttinger Universitätsreden 1974), Göttingen 1976, p. 7f.

12 Jürgen Kocka, *Nation und Gesellschaft. Historische Überlegungen zur 'deutschen Frage'*, lecture given on 17 June 80, printed (as a manuscript) by the

Bielefeld Civic Authorities. Kocka ranks the 'certain degree of legitimacy' of the state as equal with 'a certain degree of solidarity' required by 'society'.

13 Kocka offers Britain as an example: 'Britain seems to me to have demonstrated, in recent years, that active national traditions can help to solve internal crises,' *ibid*.

14 This is not contradicted by the high publication figures for the books on Prussia written by Hans-Joachim Schoeps and the success of the radio series *Preussen: Portrait einer politischen Kultur*, later published as an anthology edited by Hans-Joachim Netzer, Munich 1968.

15 Ingrid Mittenzwei, *Friedrich II von Preussen. Eine Biographie*, Berlin (East) 1979, quotation here taken from the West German licensed edition, Cologne 1980, p. 211.

16 Ingrid Mittenzwei dismisses 'left-wing' approaches as follows:

> After all the legends woven around the figure of Frederick II by the forces of German reaction, the latest version is now being presented to us by Federal Republican writers. They profess to have discovered the 'left-wing' Frederick who – of course – also stuck to order and discipline in his state. Whilst there are still these kind of 'discoveries' being made, and as long as Prussia does not belong to the past, any historical attention to Frederick II will require one to take on contemporary tasks.

Ibid., p. 211ff. Equally critical, particularly with regard to Haffner and Engelmann is: Arno Klönne, 'Gräber und Ausgräber – Die Rehabilitierung Preussens', in *Bildung und Politik*, part 6, 1980, p. 29ff.

17 Above all: Reinhard Rürup, 'Messlatte Demokratie', in *Journal für Geschichte*, vol. 1, 1979, part 5, p.52.

18 Coined by Ludwig von Rochau, *Grundsätze der Realpolitik*, Stuttgart 1853.

19 Christian Graf von Krockow, *Warnung vor Preussen*, Berlin 1981, p. 19ff.

20 *Preussen. Portrait einer politischen Kultur, p. 204.*

21 Suggested also by a remark made by former federal president Karl Carstens in his address to the 111th Meeting of the Bremen *Tabak-Kollegium* on 8 June 1980: 'But concern with Prussian history also seems especially important to me because it is noticeable that the other German State, the GDR, is turning its attention increasingly towards Prussian history.' *Loc cit*, p. 18.

22 Reinhart Koselleck, *Preussen zwischen Reform und Revolution. Allgemeines Landrecht, Verwaltung und soziale Bewegung von 1791 bis 1848*, 2nd edn, Stuttgart 1975, p. 23.

23 Introduction to Dirk Blasius' *Preussen in der deutschen Geschichte* (Neue Wissenschaftliche Bibliothek III), Königstein/Taunus 1980, p. 22.

24 Title of 5 January 1981 edition of *Der Spiegel*.

25 Hans-Ulrich Wehler, 'Preussen ist wieder chic. Der Obrigkeitsstaat im Goldrähmchen', in *Der Monat*, 31.Jg., 1979, part 3, p. 95.

26 *Ibid.*, p. 96.

27 Cf. my essay 'Das schwierige Vaterland. Geschichte und Geschichtsbewusstsein als Problem der Deutschen', in *Aus Politik und Zeitgeschichte*. Beilage zur Wochenzeitung Das parlament vom 10 Nov. 1979, p. 12.

28 This is the sort of risk run by Martin Greiffenhagen in *Die Aktualität Preussens*, pp. 70f and 146.

29 For this reason, the title of Christian Graf von Krockow's book *Warnung vor Preussen* (*Warning Against Prussia*), is somewhat misleading. Warning should be given against Prussia-clichés!

30 Blasius comments on the discussion of Prussia during the Weimar period: 'The memory of the old Prussia which was kept alive in large sections of the middle classes cut off much of the new Prussia's life-blood . . . The end of democratic Prussia was pre-planned by those who were fond of referring to the values of so-called Prussiandom.' *Preussen*, p. 37f.

31 This does not apply in the same way to the GDR, which is more ill at ease than the FRG and which – for various reasons – is more artificial. As a result, it shows stronger signs, internal and external, of Prussian character. This is felt particularly strongly by its Polish neighbours, who are fond of calling the GDR 'Red Prussia'.

32 On the plan for the 'Prussia' exhibition, see Martin Schlenke, 'Preussen fur alle. Zur Ausstellung in Berlin 1981', in *Journal für Geschichte*, Jg. 1, 1979, part 2, p. 41ff; on the plan's discussion see the 'Forum' in *ibid.*, part 5, esp. p. 48f.

33 Explanations are given in the comprehensive Exhibition Catalogue.

34 It is in this sense that Dirk Blasius describes Prussia as 'a kind of guiding sector in the formation process of modern German society'. *Loc cit.*, p. 10.

35 Cf. Barbara Vogel's introduction to the anthology edited by her, *Preussische Reformen 1807–1820*, Königstein/Taunus, 1980, p. 18.

Index